MIGHT COULD MAKE A BOOK

How to Write, Illustrate, and Publish Your Children's Picture Book

CHRISTINE NISHIYAMA

might could

Also by Christine Nishiyama

Happy Paws *(Layla and the Bots #1)*
written by Vicky Fang, published by Scholastic

Built for Speed *(Layla and the Bots #2)*
written by Vicky Fang, published by Scholastic

Cupcake Fix *(Layla and the Bots #3)*
written by Vicky Fang, published by Scholastic

Making Waves *(Layla and the Bots #4)*
written by Vicky Fang, published by Scholastic

We are Fungi*, published by Might Could Studios*

Sketchbook to Style*: Discover Your Artistic Style in Your Sketchbook, published by Might Could Studios*

Published by Might Could Studios
PO Box 92, Boone, NC 28607
www.might-could.com
First Edition
ISBN 978-0-9994039-2-1 (Print)

The first version of the content in this book was released as a pair of online classes in 2014, taken by over 14,000 students. A few years later I formed a private artists group called Might Could Beta Books which built on the content from those courses as we each worked together to create our own books. My first book *We Are Fungi,* was created within that group. I am forever thankful to those artists and friends.

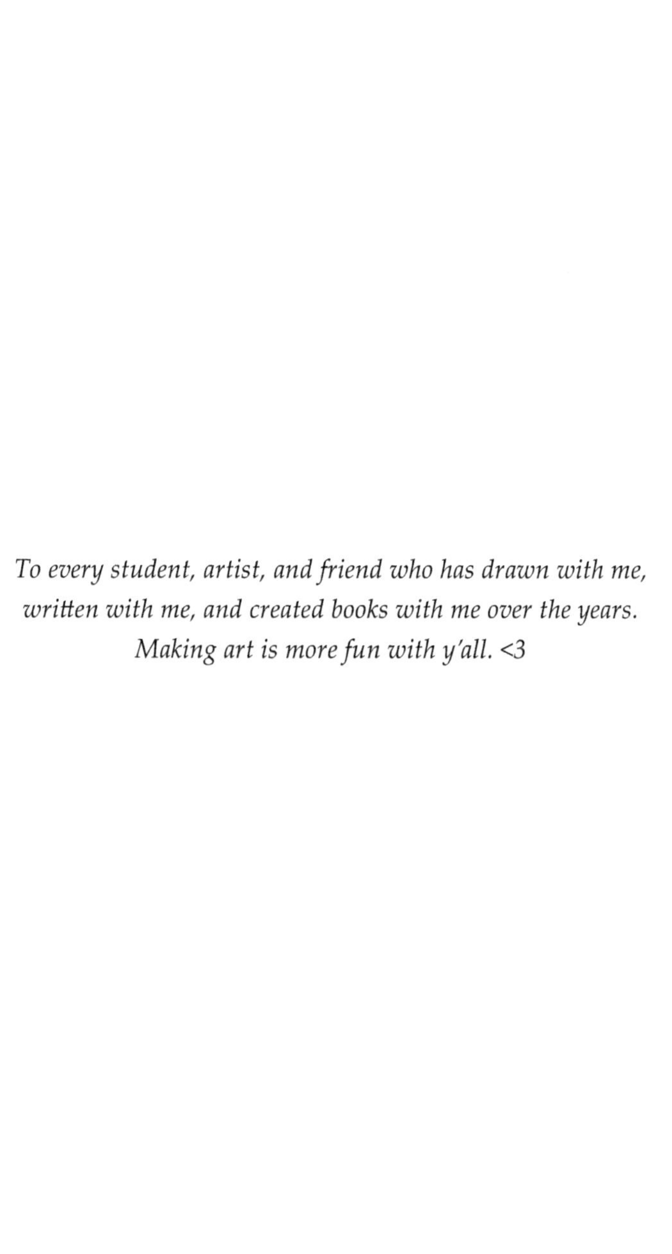

To every student, artist, and friend who has drawn with me, written with me, and created books with me over the years. Making art is more fun with y'all. <3

CONTENTS

Introduction . . . xi

Chapter 1: Intro to Picture Books . . . 1

Chapter 2: Elements of a Picture Book . . . 9

Chapter 3: Illustration Terminology . . . 15

Chapter 4: Plot Structure . . . 21

Chapter 5: How to Storyboard Your Plot . . . 27

Chapter 6: Point of View . . . 31

Chapter 7: Rhythm + Rhyme . . . 35

Chapter 8: Character Design (Writing) . . . 41

Chapter 9: Book Title + Blurb . . . 45

Chapter 10: Making a Writer's Dummy . . . 49

Chapter 11: The First Page . . . 53

Chapter 12: The Last Page . . . 57

Chapter 13: Refining a Weak Manuscript . . . 61

Chapter 14: Character Design (Drawing) . . . 69

Chapter 15: Types of PB Illustrations . . . 75

Chapter 16: Drawing a Storyboard . . . 79

Chapter 17: Refining a Storyboard . . . 87

Chapter 18: Creating Sample Spreads . . . 95

Chapter 19: Submitting Your Book to Publishers . . . 103

Chapter 20: Creating the Final Artwork . . . 111

Chapter 21: Creating the Final Book Design File 117

Chapter 22: Designing the Book Cover 123

Chapter 23: Marketing Your Book 127

Chapter 24: Self-Publishing Options 137

Chapter 25: Printing + Publishing Setup 143

Chapter 26: Book Launch Promotion. 149

Chapter 27: You Made a Book! 155

Resources 159

Further Reading 161

Templates 167

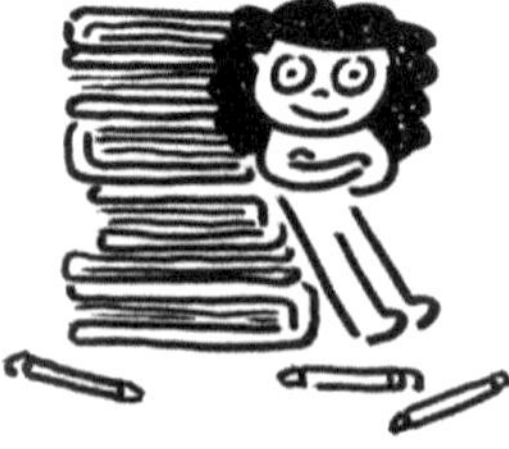

INTRODUCTION

Hi! I'm Christine Nishiyama, illustrator and writer at Might Could Studios. I make books, write essays, and draw in my sketchbook. I've kept a sketchbook drawing practice for over 20 years and have been a full-time, professional artist for over 10 years.

Over the past decade, I've taught more than 100,000 aspiring and established artists, helping them learn new skills, grow their confidence, and make more art. Many of my online classes focus on specific art techniques and processes, like composition and gesture drawing. But my true passion is creating illustrated books. Making books combines all of my loves: drawing, writing, and designing. My two classes on picture book writing and illustrating have been taken by over 14,000 students. But a lot has happened since I created those two classes in 2014!

In 2017, I self-published my first book *We Are Fungi,* a children's picture book about the kingdom of fungi. In 2019 I signed a book deal with Scholastic and in 2020, *Happy Paws (Layla and the Bots #1)* written by Vicky Fang, was published. The second, third, and fourth books in that series followed in 2020-2022. I am currently working on the final art for my next book, *We Are Jellyfish*.

And so, with all that new experience and knowledge I learned on the job and in the real world, I decided to revisit the content from my picture book classes. The book you're reading now combines all the information from those classes, updated with professional expertise. Here, I outline my authentic book-making process for you to follow as you create your own picture book.

Using my *We Are Fungi* book as an example, I show you every step from idea to manuscript to storyboard to final art to publishing (both submitting to traditional publishers and self-publishing.)

It took me years to create *We Are Fungi*. I had to scrape together all the skills and knowledge I could from books, classes, videos, and expensive professional events. And much of that content was far out of date, created before print-on-demand, email marketing, and even Photoshop existed. The rest of it, I had to figure out myself.

So, in this book, I'm sharing everything I know about making picture books: writing, illustrating, traditional publishing, self-publishing, printing, and marketing. It's all here in one place, so you don't have to waste your precious creative time searching when you could be writing and drawing.

Making a book is a big project and requires time, discipline, and dedication of us. It can be both a joy and a slog. And that is where I find the Might Could mindset becomes helpful. The phrase *might could* is Southern slang which means you may be able to do something in the future. As in, if I were to ask you: "Are you going to make your own picture book?" You would respond: "I don't know, but I *might could*!"

Call it redundant and bad grammar if you like. But to me, it represents a realistically optimistic point of view. Making a picture book is hard work, and who knows what will happen, but gosh darn it, let's give it a go.

You never know what might could happen!

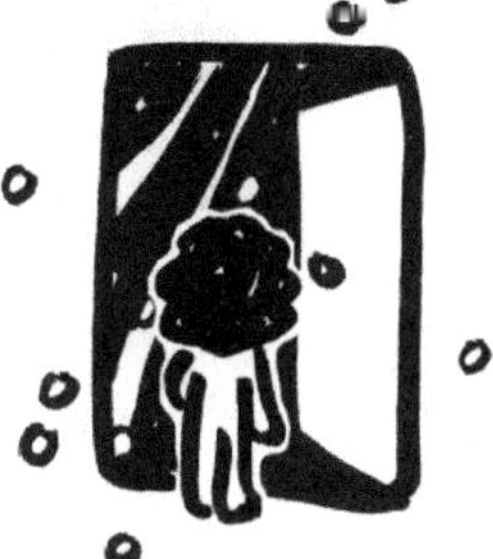

CHAPTER 1

INTRO TO PICTURE BOOKS

What is a Picture Book?

Let's start at the beginning and define some terms. A *picture book* combines words and pictures in a book format to tell a story to young children. The target audience is children from ages 2–8.

Picture Books vs. Illustrated Books

A picture book is different than an *illustrated book,* such as a middle-grade chapter book. In a picture book, the illustrations are vital to the story and a text cannot be fully understood without them. In an illustrated book, the illustrations are supplemental to a text that can stand on its own.

WildWood by Colin Meloy and Carson Ellis is an example of an illustrated book. It's structured like a chapter book, the illustrations are not necessarily on every page and are sometimes small spot illustrations (see Chapter 3 for more on Illustration Terminology).

Where the Wild Things Are by Maurice Sendak is an example of a picture book. In this book there is less text, and the illustrations partner with the words to help tell the full story instead of just reiterating the story.

What's the Purpose of Children's Books?

Picture books are the first stage of learning to read. They are intended to be read together: one person who can read and one person who cannot read. As the parent or older reader reads the words, the younger child can "read" the pictures while listening to words, learning the meaning of words and language.

Early reader picture books can also help a child learn to read on their own. Picture books place value on rich storytelling and the joy of reading. They can be fun, silly, educational, deep, and thought-provoking.

What's NOT the Purpose of Children's Books?

A picture book should *not* aim to overtly teach lessons or morals. Children understand more than adults typically give them credit for. Rich stories inherently deal with values and character—it isn't necessary to blatantly state a moral at the end like, "And then little Johnny knew sharing his toys was the right thing to do."

If you want to make a picture book, your job is to be a writer/illustrator, not a teacher. Don't begin this process with the intention of teaching a lesson—start with the intention of telling a good story. Quality storytelling leaves room for readers to piece together and interpret the story's meaning themselves.

Picture Book Audiences

Child and Adult Readers

Your primary picture book audience is a child between 2 and 8. But the person reading the book to that child could be a parent, grandparent, teacher, librarian… any adult or older child who can read! The adults are also the ones buying your book, so it's wise to make the book appealing to them as well.

Readability

A picture book should be fairly easy to read out loud. This doesn't necessarily mean simple, it's more about rhythm, flow, and how the words sound out loud. We'll cover more about this in Chapters 6 and 7. For now, you goal should be write a story an adult won't mind reading again and again.

Words + Pictures Working Together

The most important aspect of a picture book is how the words and pictures work together. The example above shows how the words and pictures can work together to tell a complete story.

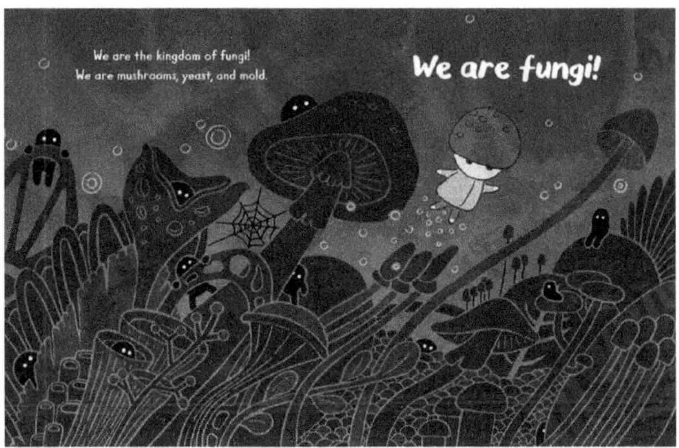

A spread from my book, *We Are Fungi.*

In my book, *We Are Fungi,* the written text tells one part of the story (the scientific, non fiction side), while the illustrations tell another part of the story (a more fictional, magical side).

Together, the words and pictures tell one complete story that could not be fully understood without both working together. This partnership allows the adult, child, and book to all be active participants in the storytelling.

Types of Children's Books

Now that we've gone over the basics of picture books, let's look at the eight different types of children's books. As you read through, think about which type of book your story may be best suited for.

Board Books

Target audience: 0–2 years
Example: *Moo, Baa, La La La!* by Sandra Boynton
Average word count: less than 300

Board books are written for very young children who can't yet read. They are made out of thick, cardboard pages to withstand the heavy handling and chewing of babies and young toddlers.

Concept Books

Target audience: ages 2–5
Average word count: less than 300
Example: *Quiet Loud* by Leslie Patricelli

Concept books introduce children to a theme such as letters, numbers, or shapes. Sometimes they tell a story and sometimes simply list items within the concept.

Picture Books

Target audience: ages 2–8
Average word count: 400–1,000
Example: *Llama, Llama, Red Pajama* by Anna Dewdney

The narrative story becomes more important in picture books. A picture book combines words and pictures to tell a story together—the pictures are necessary for the full story to be understood. A child can "read" the pictures as their parent/teacher reads the words, learning the meaning of words and language.

Non-Fiction Picture Books

Target audience: 3–12 years
Average word count: 400–1,000
Example: *The Big Book of Bugs* by Yuval Zommer

These books introduce children to new educational concepts in a fun and easy-to-understand way. They lean towards the informational, but often include some sort of narrative story as well.

Wordless Picture Books

Target audience: 2–12 years
Average word count: 0!
Example: *Journey* by Aaron Becker

These stories are told completely by illustrations—there are no words. The lack of written text allows the child to expand and interpret the full story in their mind to go along with pictures. It also allows children who can't yet read to read a book on their own.

Early Readers

Target audience: 5–8 years
Average word count: 2,000
Example: *Green Eggs and Ham* by Dr. Seuss

Also known as Easy Readers or Beginner Books, these books help children learn to read on their own, growing their confidence and abilities. These books have more text and are often longer than Picture Books, but still have illustrations on every page.

Early Reader Graphic Novels

Target audience: 5+ years
Average word count: 2,000
Example: *Narwhal Unicorn of the Sea!* by Ben Clanton

These books are told in comic form with pages broken up into panels and dialogue often in speech bubbles. They help children learn to read on their own. Perfect for more visual-minded children and reluctant readers.

Chapter Books

Target audience: 7-10 years
Average word count: 4,000–12,000
Example: *Ivy + Bean,* by Annie Barrows and Sophie Blackall

Chapter books are structured in paragraphs and chapters, similar to adult novels. There are illustrations throughout the book, though not necessarily on every page. The illustrations can be full-page, half-page, or small spots. The pictures mainly reiterate what is communicated in the text.

CHAPTER 2

ELEMENTS OF A PICTURE BOOK

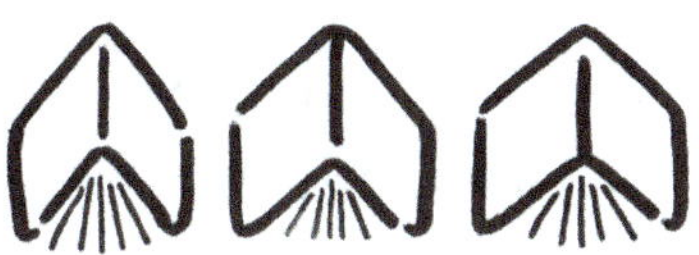

Picture Book Standards

Page Size

The size of a picture book varies widely depending on the book type, age range, and how much money you or your publisher are willing to spend. The important thing to consider is that if you plan on submitting your book to publishers or self-publishing and selling your book through an online marketplace (Amazon, Ingram, etc), you'll have to adhere to the standards they accept.

You don't have to decide on the final size of your book until you begin making the sample spreads (covered in Chapter 18). For now, you can begin thinking about whether you want your book to be formatted as landscape (horizontal), portrait (vertical), or square. Start paying attention to how existing books are oriented.

Page Count

A picture book is typically 32 pages long. This is standard because in offset printing the pages are printed in multiples of 4 (called a *signature*) and then folded and bound together into the book. If your book's page count is a not multiple of 4 (ie. 28, 32, 36, etc), blank pages are added until it is a multiple of 4. This is why you often see blank pages in books, even adult novels—they're filling out the signatures.

This multiple of 4 rule goes for all types of books, except for board books or spiral-bound books, which are not printed in signatures.

What happens if you create a book not following this rule? It's not a huge deal. You'll just have an extra 1-3 blank pages in the front or back of your book. Also keep in mind, especially if self-publishing, more pages means more expensive printing. Some picture books are longer than 32 pages, but most fit within this guideline.

Word Count

Word count varies greatly depending on what type of children's book you're making, but here are some general guidelines:

- **Board Book:** less than 300
- **Concept Book:** less than 300
- **Picture Book:** 400–1000
- **Early Readers:** 2,000
- **Chapter Book:** 4,000–12,000

Picture Book Anatomy

Now let's look at the parts of a picture book. I'm going to use a storyboard layout so you can see all the elements of the book in one flat image.

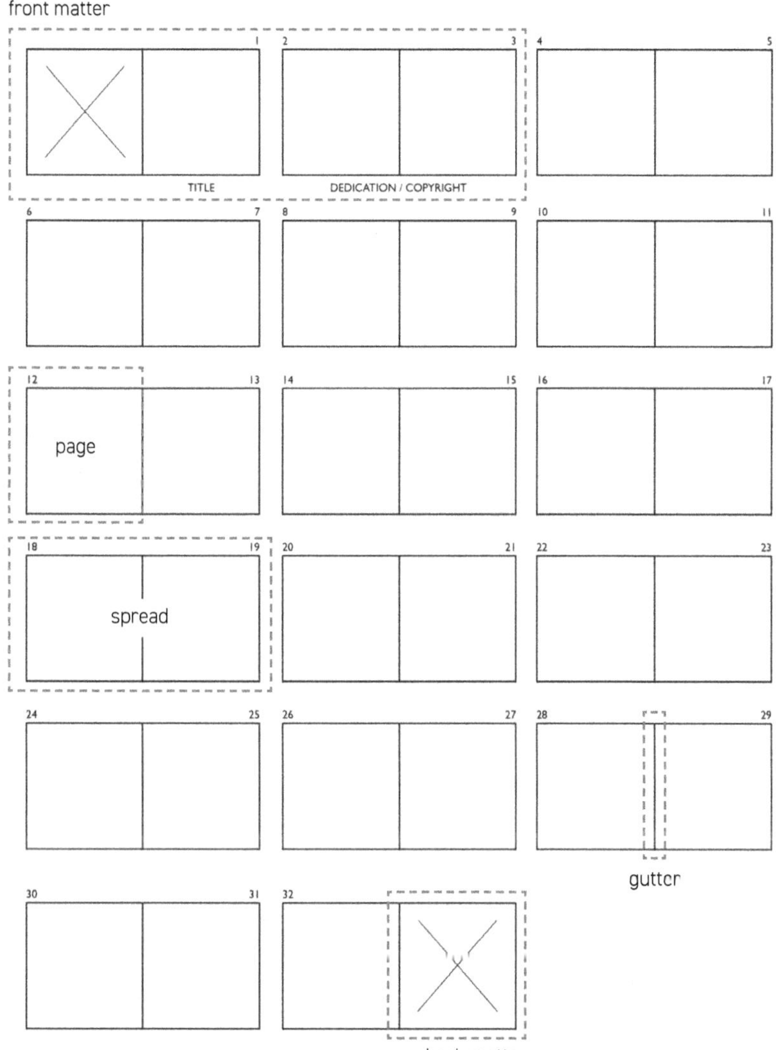
front matter
1
2
3
4
5
TITLE
DEDICATION / COPYRIGHT
6
7
8
9
10
11
12
13
14
15
16
17
page
18
19
20
21
22
23
spread
24
25
26
27
28
29
gutter
30
31
32
back matter

Front Matter

First, we have the front matter. This includes everything in the book before the actual story starts, which is usually around page 4 or 6. The front matter can include any or all of the following: full title, half-title, author, illustrator, dedication, publisher, copyright info, editor, art director, and publication date.

Pages

This is a single page. As I mentioned before, there are typically 32 pages in a picture book.

Spreads

Two pages together form a spread, as seen here. The number of spreads in a book can vary depending on how the front matter is laid out and how many pages are necessary. A book with 12-16 spreads is normal, but it can be more or less.

Gutter

The gutter is the place in the middle of each spread where the two pages meet the binding. When illustrating a picture book, the gutter has to be taken into consideration to avoid things getting clipped or lost in the gutter.

Back Matter

The back matter includes the author's notes if there are any. Usually, non-fiction picture books will have an author's note to further explain some of the material or history in the book, or how the author researched the subject.

Endpapers

The endpapers are the two pages in the front and back of the book, usually glued to the binding. Endpapers can be solid colored paper or have patterns or illustrations printed on them.

Artistic Influences

All artists all influenced by other artists. It's helpful to be aware of who and what you are influenced by, both broadly as an artist, and specifically with this book you're working on right now. Throughout the process, when you feel stuck or lost (which *will* happen!) you'll have your list of influential books and artists to turn to. They'll help jog your memory of what your original idea was, spark your imagination for what to do, and inspire new ideas and paths forward.

Not sure who or what your artistic influences are? Think back to the books you loved as a kid. What was your favorite book to read as a child? What memories of books do you have? Why do you remember them? The illustrations? The story? The words? Revisit and read those stories again if you can and add them to your list! You can also find a list of award-winning and timeless picture books at the end of this book if you need somewhere to start.

This influence list doesn't have to just include children's book makers, I often include painters, graphic novelists, and musicians as well. Creating a playlist that fits the mood I'm shooting for with a book has been especially helpful for me with my most recent book. Listening to it while I make the final art helps remind me of the essence of the book. As your making your book, add any songs you hear that feel like your book to this playlist. It will continue to grow and evolve as your book does!

We Are Fungi Influence Music

Fog, Nosaj Thing
Ethereal, Nosaj Thing
Virus, Bjork
Crystalline, Bjork
Shoouss Lullaby, Teebs
Drift, Ratatat

CHAPTER 3

ILLUSTRATION TERMINOLOGY

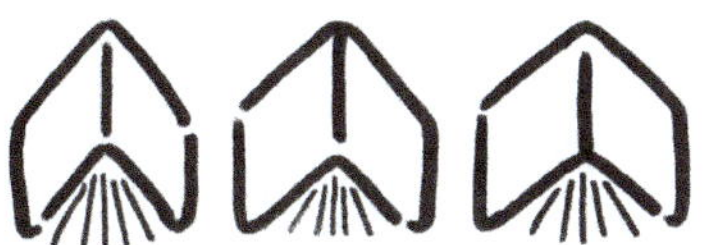

Before we jump into the first steps of crafting your story, there are some illustration terms and concepts you should know about.

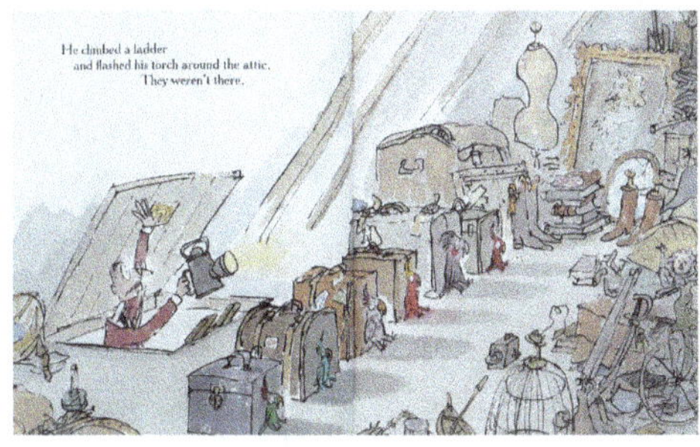

Decalage

Example: *Cockatoo,* by Quentin Blake

Decalage means the disparity between word and image—the words say one thing, while the picture says another. Above, in *Cockatoo,* a man is looking for his birds. The words on this spread say: "He climbed a ladder and flashed his torch around the attic. They weren't there." But the reader can clearly see there are six cockatoos behind the suitcases! Children love to be able to point out the difference and read the "true" story through the pictures.

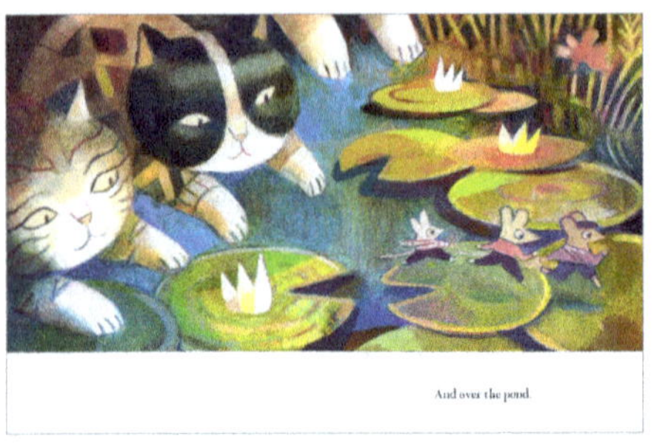

Composition

Ex: *Mina,*
by Matthew Forsythe

Composition refers to how the different elements of an picture book spread are arranged in relation to each other. In general, the illustrations in a picture book should lead you through the book, from left to right on each spread, and from page to page.

This can be done subtly by organizing the elements in your composition from left to right. Or it can be done more obviously, by having a character run across the page from left to right, for example. In this spread from *Mina* above, almost every element is composed to guide the reader's eyes from left to right. We'll talk about how to do this in Chapter 16: Drawing a Storyboard.

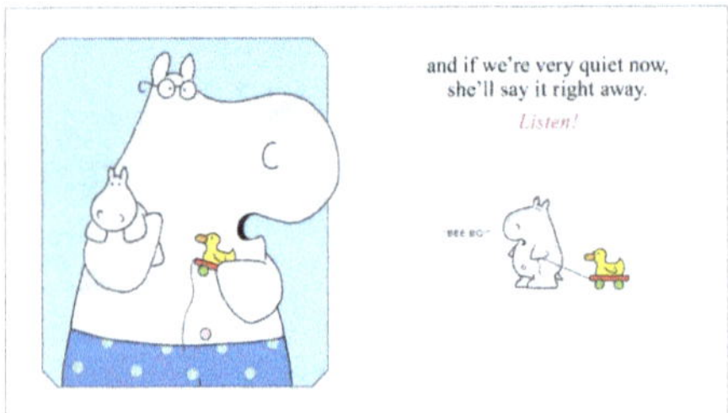

Color + White Space

Ex: *Belly Button Book!*
by Sandra Boynton

Color and white space can quickly communicate emotion and mood. White space is also a way to focus the readers attention on a specific element. In *Belly Button Book!*, pastel colors set a fun, lighthearted mood, while the use of white space calls out the little hippo right when his time to speak comes.

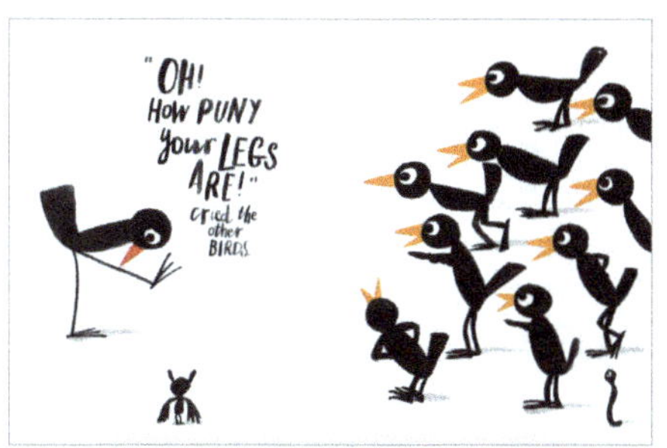

Typography

Ex: *Bob the Artist*
by Marion Deuchars

Because the combination of words and pictures is the essence of picture books, typography is a vital element of their design and can communicate a great deal about the story. The text can be typeset in traditional stanzas, like poetry, or it can be more fluidly aligned with the illustrations, becoming part of the picture itself.

In *Bob the Artist*, the typography is all hand-painted, integrating it into the overall artwork and adding an extra punch of emotion.

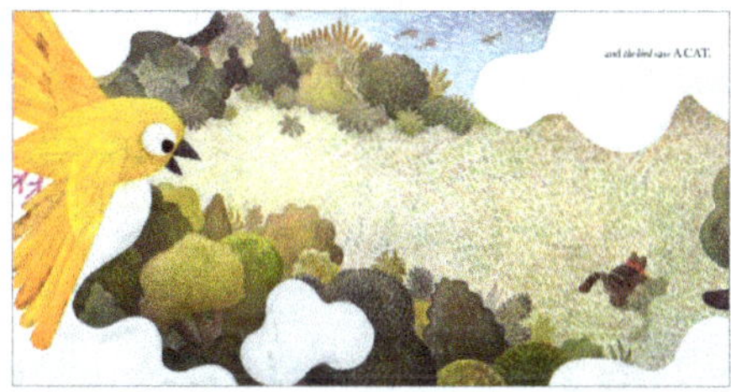

Perspective

Ex: *They All Saw a Cat*
by Brendan Wenzel

The chosen perspective, or point of view, of an illustration can also communicate important pieces of the story. If the reader looks down on a character, that character is perceived as timid, doubtful, or scared. If the reader looks up at a character, that character is perceived as brave, excited, or determined. Cropping the artwork to a close shot, or zooming out to a wide shot also affect the mood.

The book, *They All Saw a Cat,* is all about perspective shifts and each spread shows the cat from a different animal's viewpoint. Above is an overhead shot of the cat from a bird's perspective.

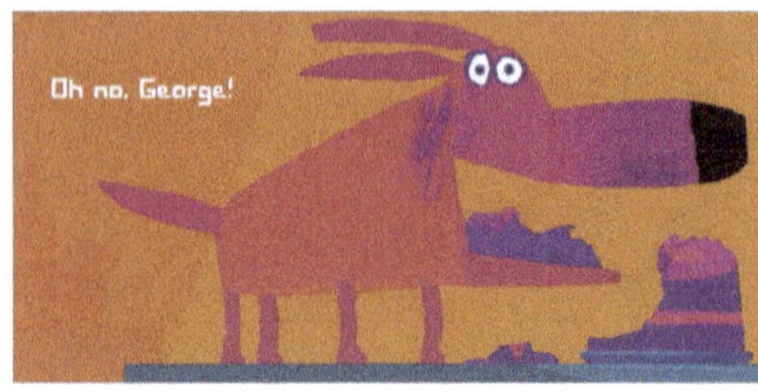

Style

Ex: *Oh No, George!*
by Chris Haughton

Picture books exist in every style imaginable. The art can be realistic or abstract, silly or serious, and everything in between! There is no best style for a picture book, and I have a very firm belief that there is no right way to make a piece of art. It's all very subjective and all you can do is make the art that feels good to *you*.

The spread above from *Oh No, George!*, shows a bold, graphic style using bright, solid colors and strong shapes.

I don't go too deep into personal artistic style in this book, but if you find yourself getting hung up on how to draw in your own way, I'd recommend checking out my book, *Sketchbook to Style: Discover your Artistic Style in Your Sketchbook*. I go much deeper there into what makes up an artistic style and how to develop your own.

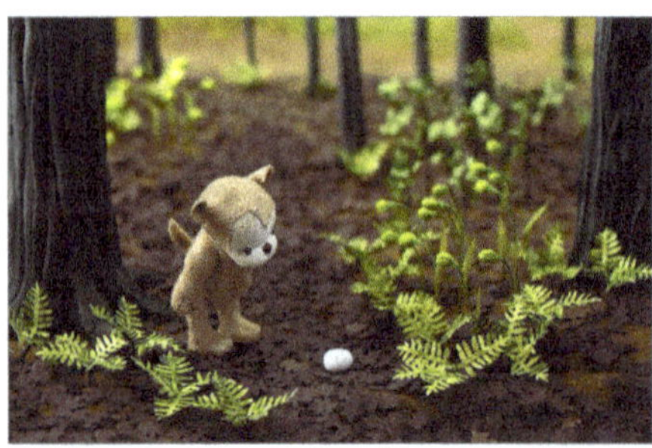

Mediums

Ex: *Hank Finds an Egg*
by Rebecca Dudley

Just like style, there is no required medium in picture books. You can use whatever art materials you like to create your illustrations! Picture books commonly use pencil, pen, ink, watercolor, oil, acrylics, collage. Almost all picture books use a digital mediums, like

Photoshop, whether for setting, type, art editing, or painting the whole thing digitally! There's no need to just choose one either—many picture books use a combination of different mediums.

Some books really think outside the box, like *Hank Finds an Egg*. In this book, the artwork was all created by hand using felt, textiles, and other physical materials. The scene was then photographed as flat illustrations and printed as spreads in a book!

There are no rules!

CHAPTER 4

PLOT STRUCTURE

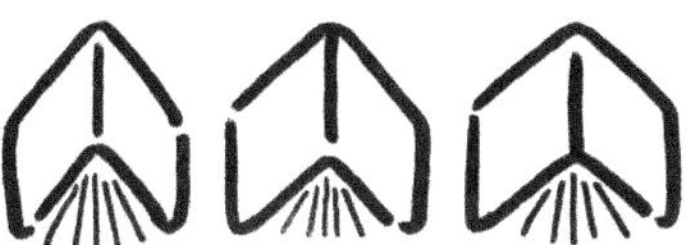

The Three-Act Plot Structure

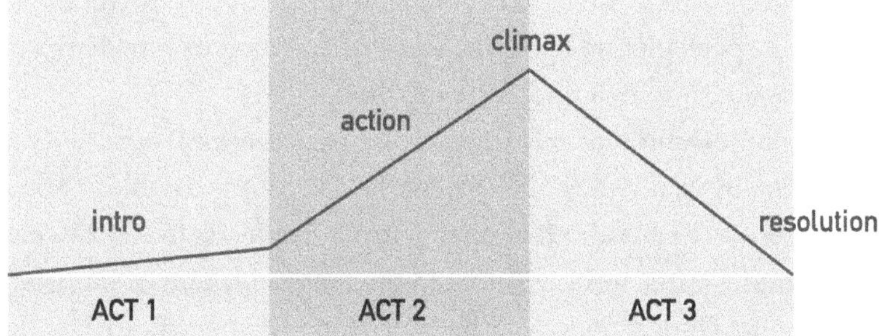

The *Three-Act Plot* is the most common plot structure for any type of story, whether a book, movie, or TV show. This structure has a beginning, middle, and end, called Acts. In Act 1, the characters and conflict are introduced. In Act 2, the action begins, the main character reaches their low point, and the action (or tension) reaches its climax. Finally, in Act 3, there is a resolution (where the tension is somewhat resolved) and loose ends are wrapped up.

Picture Book Plot Structures

The Three-Act plot is commonly used in picture books, but there are a number of other plot structures that are often used instead of the Three-Act plot or in combination with it. Let's look at some of them now!

Classic

This is the common three-act plot with a clear beginning, middle, end. A very basic and common three-plot picture book story goes something like this: the story's main character has a problem, they encounter three obstacles (or attempt three times to solve the problem), the character is demoralized and hits their low point, which leads to one final attempt to solve the problem, they successfully solve the problem, and the story resolves. The word "problem" here could also be replaced with "desire" or "want", as the character strives to fill that desire. Every character must want something!

In a 32-page picture book, the story's resolution usually happens on pages 30-31, with a final wrap-up on page 32.

A good example of this Classic plot structure is *Where the Wild Things Are* by Maurice Sendak. In Act 1, Max causes trouble at home and is sent to bed without supper (intro). This leads to Act 2, when Max's room shifts and he is now in the magical island of monsters called Wild Things. Soon Max becomes king (rising action), lets the power go to his head, and sends the Wild Things to bed without supper. Max then enters his low point and feels lonely. He decides to go home, but the Wild Things don't want him to go and throw tantrums (climax). In Act 3, Max sails home, slips into his bedroom and finds his hot supper waiting for him (resolution).

Circular

A Circular plot structure begins and ends at the same place. This can be achieved in many different ways, and can be overt or subtle.

It could be that the story begins and ends in the same setting after a journey in between, or a character could look the same at the beginning and end with changes in between, or the book could begin and end with the same sentence.

A good example of Circular plot structure is *If You Give a Mouse a Cookie* by Laura Numeroff and Felicia Bond. The story begins by giving a mouse to a cookie. The mouse asks for a glass of milk to drink with it, and then keeps requesting more and more things as the story goes on. By the end of the story, the mouse asks for a glass of milk and then finally, a cookie to go with it, coming full circle back to where the story began.

Concept

A Concept plot prioritizes the introduction of exploration of a topic or category to children. These books can have a narrative story, or can be mostly informational.

A great example of a Concept book is Shapes Trilogy by Mac Barnett and Jon Klassen, including *Triangle, Circle,* and *Square.* These three books each have a narrative story, but their focus is on teaching young kids about concept of shapes (triangles, circles, and squares) and the concept of size (small, medium, and large).

Cumulative

In a Cumulative plot, each time a new event occurs, the previous events in the story are repeated. This leads to a very predictable book (which young readers love as they can guess what comes next), but the author usually adds a twist at the end to break the repetition and add surprise.

A good example of a Cumulative book is *The Napping House* by Audrey Wood and Don Wood. The story begins with a house "where everyone is sleeping", then a bed, a granny, a child, a dog, and on and on, repeating "where everyone is sleeping" as each sleeping thing, person, or animal is added. Eventually, a flea who is *not* sleeping is added, breaking the pattern and waking everyone up. The pattern then reverses, and the story takes us back through each cumulative thing.

Mirror

In a Mirror plot, the second half of the story echoes what occurred in the first half of the story.

An example of a Mirror book is *A Sick Day for Amos McGee* by Philip C. Stead and Erin E. Stead. The story details Amos McGee's typical day working at the zoo as he visits the elephant first, then the tortoise, the penguin, the rhino, and lastly, the owl. But one day, Amos wakes up sick and can't go to the zoo. So, the animals board the bus and visit Amos in the same order as before: elephant, tortoise, penguin, rhino, and owl, mirroring the first half of the book.

Parallel

In a Parallel plot, two storylines take place at the same time. This is sometimes called Dual Narrative. Usually the storylines are related or similar and often come together somehow in the end.

A good example of a Parallel plot is *Where's Mommy?* by Beverly Donofrio and Barbara McClintock. This book follows the two storylines of a girl and mouse searching for their mother at bedtime. They are both in their separate bedrooms, and begin looking in corresponding rooms for their mothers. The girl looks in the human kitchen, while the mouse looks in the mouse kitchen and so on. The artwork shows these storylines happening simultaneously on the same page.

Reversal

In a Reversal plot, the character and/or plot is portrayed in a way that is opposite from what you would expect. It flips some common concept on its head and considers what the reversal would be like.

A great example of a Reversal book is *Children Make Terrible Pets* by Peter Brown. A normal picture book about pets would be a story of a child having an animal for a pet. But this book shows the reverse: a story of an animal having a child for a pet! In this case, a bear attempts to bring a little boy home to keep as a pet.

Experimenting with Your Plot Structure

Once you begin writing your story, it can be helpful to look back at these plot structures and try reorganizing your story in different ways to see what works best. One story could be told in any number of plot structures, and experimenting is the best way to find the one (or combination!) that fits your story!

You also do not have to follow any of these plot structures or you can follow one very loosely. These structures don't have to be cages for your story. You might find they offer nice tidy scaffolds for your story, but if it's not working remember: you can always break free and do something completely new!

CHAPTER 5

HOW TO STORYBOARD YOUR PLOT

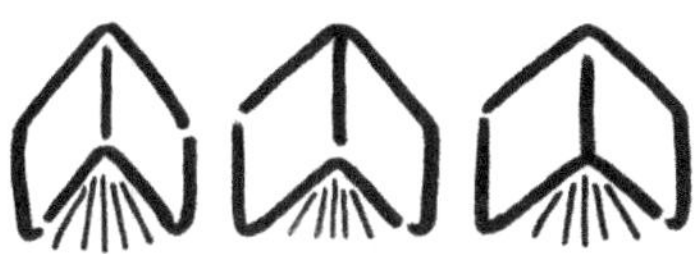

You can use a storyboard format to help you expand your story idea out into a full plot or test your existing plot to see if it fits in a typical picture book format. It works best if you work in a sketchbook, notebook, or piece of paper.

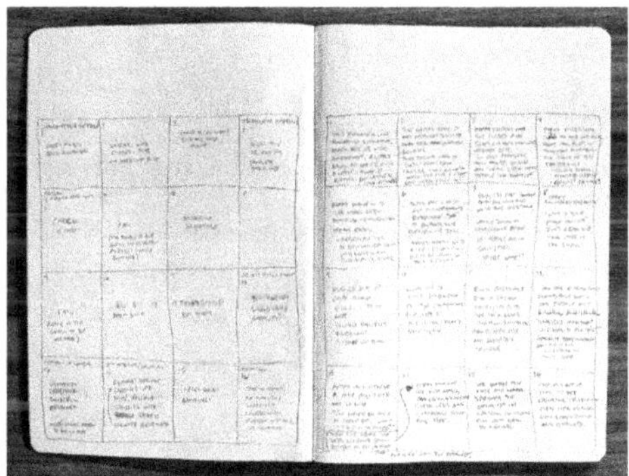

First, draw a chart with 16 squares, 4 across and 4 down, like in the example above. Each of these boxes represents one spread in your book (16 spreads = 32 pages). Now in each box, write out a simple plot point from your story. Something short like "Oni walked to the dog park." Do this for each plot point in your story, filling out the story to fit in these 16 boxes.

Don't expect to get this right on the first try! It takes a lot of experimenting and moving things around to find the right order and pace for a story. Take your time and be patient. Make as many plot storyboards as you need to mold your story into the picture book format.

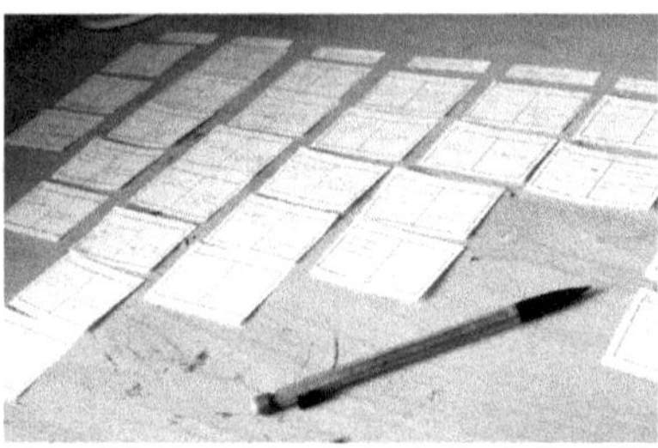

Another helpful exercise is to cut up your plot storyboard and move around the spreads on your desk, allowing you to try new arrangements and make small adjustments without redrawing the whole storyboard.

After you've gotten a grasp on the order and pace of your plot, you can begin to refine the outline by expanding the content in each box. Take your most recent storyboard plot, and redraw it, but this time, write a little more detail about what happens, instead of just a plot point. This is a great way to begin the actual writing process because it helps you plan and focus on the plot rather than on individual words or specifics. It also feels low pressure and not as daunting as starting on a blank page!

Example Plot Storyboard

If you're struggling with expanding and pacing out your story, it can be helpful to look at a typical plot outline of a picture book and think of how the pieces of your story could fit together.

I've created a sample picture book plot storyboard below with the pieces of a classic plot structure. But please keep in mind: your story does *not* have to fit into this structure! This is just an example and is one of many options. These are not rules, and not every picture book will or should fit into this outline. But this is a good place to start if it's your first time writing a picture book.

introduce characters + action	*introduce characters + action*	*set up conflict/desire*	*set up conflict/desire*
obstacle /action #1	*obstacle /action #1*	*obstacle /action #1*	*obstacle /action #2*
obstacle /action #2	*obstacle /action #2*	*Low Point*	*obstacle /action #3*
obstacle /action #3	*Climax*	*Resolution*	*Wrap Up*

Try making a new plot storyboard fitting your plot points into my version of the class structure above. Does this help you pace out your story? How could you rearrange or change the structure to work better with your story? What would happen if you tried out one of the other plot structures? If you only had one obstacle in mind, what could two other obstacles be? Or if you have three, what would happen if you only had one?

Experiment, experiment, experiment! And remember, writing a story takes time. It's not going to all fall into place without you putting in the time and effort to get there. Enjoy the ride, be curious, and see what happens!

CHAPTER 6

POINT OF VIEW

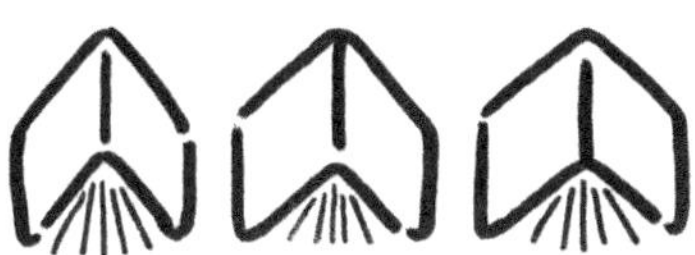

Point of View (POV) has a major impact on how your story is told and a change in POV can drastically change your story. As you are working on writing your story, a good exercise is to rewrite it in a different POV, just to see what it changes. You might be surprised!

Let's take a look at the three most common types of POV.

Third Person, Single POV

Third Person, Single is the most common POV in picture books. An outside narrator (meaning not a character in the story) tells the story from one character's perspective. The narrator only knows what the character already knows, as it happens.

If we were writing a story about a dog named Oni, an example of Third Person, Single POV could be:

"Oni looked out into the beautiful Blue Ridge Mountains."

The narrator is an outside voice and is simply describing with Oni sees or does.

Third Person, Omniscient POV

In Third Person, Omniscient, an outside narrator (not a character in the story) tells the story, but this narrator knows the story from multiple or all characters' perspectives.

Using our dog story, an example could be:

"Oni looked out into the beautiful Blue Ridge mountains. His friend Lucy was hiding behind the bushes."

See how this narrator can see more than the main character can? This narrator knows and can tell us that Lucy is hiding in the bushes even though Oni does not know that she is there. The narrator can see everything and knows everything.

First Person POV

In First Person, the narrator is an active character in the story, and uses the words "I" and "we" in telling the story. This allows us to write more deeply about the emotion of the character, but also limits us to only write about what is experienced by that particular character.

Using our dog story, an example could be:

"I looked out into the beautiful Blue Ridge Mountains."

Now Oni is the main character *and* the narrator. The story is told from Oni's perspective in his own voice.

Second Person POV

Second Person is the most rare POV. Here, the narrator addresses the reader of the book using the word "you". This draws the reader into the story as a participant or even character. It can be difficult to tell a story in Second Person and is almost always paired with another POV, but it's an interesting experiment to try!

Using our dog story, here are a few different examples:

"You looked out into the beautiful mountains and saw Oni."
Second Person (you)

"I looked out into the beautiful mountains and saw you."
First Person (I) + Second Person (you)

"Oni looked out into the beautiful mountains and saw you."
Third Person, Single (Oni) + Second Person (you)

"Oni looked out into the beautiful mountains but did not see you."
Third Person, Omniscient (Oni) + Second Person (you)

Now the reader is involved in the story and integrated into the action and events!

Experimenting with POV

All of those examples tell the same plot point quite differently! Some POVs feel factual and straight-forward, some feel emotional and individual, and some feel kind of creepy!

Try rewriting your story using a different POV and see how it changes the way your story is told or how it feels. Which fits your story best? You never know until you try!

CHAPTER 7

RHYTHM + RHYME

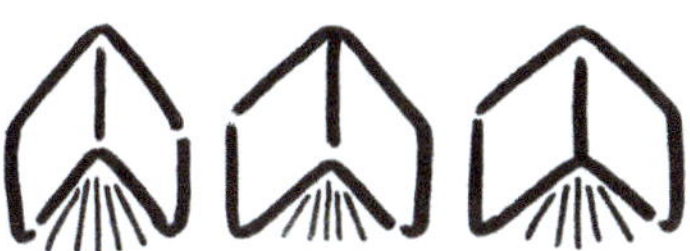

You Don't Have to Rhyme!

During lectures while attending Society of Children's Book Writers and Illustrators (SCBWI) conferences, I heard over and over from editors that they decline almost all the rhyming manuscripts they receive. They reported that this wasn't because rhyming books are unpopular or unwanted—everyone love rhyming books. It's because rhyming is *hard*. And most people are bad at it.

I'm still studying and learning the elements of rhyming, so I'm not going to pretend to be an expert on it. But these editors shared with us the big problem with rhyme: if you haven't deeply studied rhyme, it's easy to get caught up in finding words that rhyme and changing your story or sentence to fit the rhyme, instead of using rhyme to enhance your story. Then you have a book that rhymes, but a story that is bland or awkward to read.

My suggestion, if you are new to making picture books and have not already studied rhyming, would be to not try to write your first book in rhyme. Instead, you can focus on learning all the other elements of writing a successful story. Then once you have more of a grasp on that, you can move on to studying rhyme and work on that with your next book.

This is just my personal suggestion though, if you feel you can make a rhyming book or just want to give it a try, then go for it! Just be sure you prioritize telling a good story first.

Either Way, Rhythm is Still Important

Whether you're rhyming or not, you still need to think about rhythm when writing your story. Here's a tip from the rhythm king, Dr. Seuss: "Shorten paragraphs and sentences, then shorten words… use verbs. Let the kids fill in the adjectives." Let's go over some of the elements and terminology of rhythm and rhyme.

Beats

As you're writing, think about the beats of your sentences. A beat is a heavily stressed syllable. Beats are more emphasized and when spoken out loud, they are naturally pronounced louder, for longer. Unstressed or lightly stressed syllables fall between beats. Here's an example (the heavy beats are in bold):

The ***dog*** *ran* ***down*** *the* ***stairs****.*

Rhythm and Mood

The number of syllables between beats is what gives a sentence its rhythm. Different rhythms have different moods. Shorter sentences with fewer syllables between beats create a quicker rhythm. This implies a fun, energetic mood. Longer sentences with more syllables between beats create a slower rhythm. This implies a more relaxed, sleepy mood.

Rhythm Patterns

Let's take a quick look at the four most common rhythm patterns: Iambic, Trochee, Dactyl, and Anapest.

" – " represents a light stress " / " represents a heavy stress

Iambic, – /

This rhythm pattern is a light stress followed by a heavy stress.
It sounds like: da DUM, da DUM, da DUM.
Ex: A | **piece** | of | **cake**

Trochee, / –

This rhythm pattern is a heavy stress followed by a light stress.
It sounds like: DUM da, DUM da, DUM da
Ex: **Dou** | ble | **Trou** | ble

Dactyl, / – –

This rhythm pattern is a heavy stress followed by two light stresses.
It sounds like: DUM da da, DUM da da, DUM da da
Ex: **Hick** | o | ry, | **dick** | or | y

Anapest, – – /

This rhythm pattern is two light stresses followed by a heavy stress
It sounds like: da da DUM, da da DUM, da da DUM
Ex: T'was | the | **night**

Poetry Techniques

Writing a picture book can be similar to writing poetry. Even if you aren't rhyming your story, you can still utilize poetry techniques. I'm going to go through and explain some of the most common techniques. You probably already know most of these, but may not have thought to consciously put them in your writing.

Using these poetry techniques can make reading more fun for both the adult and child. Children also enjoy the repetition and repeating it themselves.

Onomatopoeia

A word that represents a sound.
Ex: Clang, bang, swoosh, buzz

Alliteration

The repetition of consonant sounds at the beginning of words.
*Ex: The **t**iny **t**urtle stared at **t**he **t**errestrial **t**ortoise.*

Assonance

The repetition of vowel sounds.
*Ex: The c**a**t in the h**a**t swung a b**a**t.*

Consonance

The repetition of consonant sounds in the middle or end of words.
*Ex: The pi**tt**er-pa**tt**er of rain.*

Personification

Giving human characteristics and personality traits to an animal or inanimate object.

Ex: The fire alarm ***screamed*** *at my burnt cookies.*

Metaphor

A comparison between two things to give a visual image.

Ex: Life is a merry-go-round with ups and downs.

Simile

A comparison between two things using the words "like" or "as".

Ex: His bones rattled ***like*** *a wind chime.*

Using Rhythm + Rhyme

Try incorporating some of these poetic techniques and rhythm patterns in your manuscript. You certainly don't have to use any of these styles of writing, but it's worth experimenting with them to see if you enjoy writing this way or how it may improve how your story reads out loud.

If you'd like to learn more about rhyming, I recommend reading and studying children's poetry anthologies such as *A Child's Anthology of Poetry,* by Elizabeth Hauge Sword and *A Child's Book of Poems* by Gyo Fujikawa.

CHAPTER 8

CHARACTER DESIGN (WRITING)

Now let's focus on developing the main character in your story. Designing a character involves more than just choosing what type of clothing they wear or how they style their hair. As a picture book creator, you need to develop the character fully, outside *and* inside.

Your Main Character Should Be...

There are a few characteristics that are present in all well-developed main characters. First, they should be relatable, meaning they have flaws just like real people do. Readers can relate much more easily to a flawed (ie. realistic) character than a perfect character, and this makes the character feel more believable. So consider: for all the good traits you character may have, what flaws do they have? How do they tend to slip up or make mistakes sometimes?

For a children's picture book, the main character is most often a child or an animal. Children can't relate as well to an adult main character. Typically, the main character is a tiny bit older than the age range of the story, allowing the child-reader to look up to them while still being able to relate to them.

The main character should also be somewhat independent and strong, although they won't necessarily start the story that way or find it easy to be that way. But almost all main characters have a story arc of solving their own problem, achieving their own desire, or coming to some important insight on their own. This doesn't mean they don't have help! But by declaring the character independent, we are saying they are not dependent on parents, adults, or anyone else to solve the conflict of their story. As the main character, they are the hero, and the one to solve the problem.

Your Main Character Should Want Something

Perhaps the most important aspect of a main character is that they *want* something. This sounds basic and simple, but it can be a vital tool in creating a interesting character and story with depth. Your characters want can also be a guiding star for your book, a phrase you can keep in mind when making decisions about what happens in your story. In other words, your characters desire provides the entire basis, motivation, and conflict of your book.

So what is it that your main character wants? Why do they want it? What is their goal? What do they have to overcome to get there? How would achieving that goal change them?

Thinking through and answering these questions will help you develop a main character that is relatable, believable, independent, strong, and unique—it will make them into a character that can fuel an entire book.

CHAPTER 9

BOOK TITLE + BLURB

Stuck and Stumped

At this point in the process of making *We Are Fungi*, I was frustrated. I was at that stage when you don't really know what book you're trying to make, and you're trying to figure everything out, and you want to make the book *so bad*, but it just won't come out, and either everything you write is terrible, or you can't write anything at all. It's a terrible feeling.

When I get stumped on where a book is going, especially in the beginning stages, I find it helpful to think about book blurbs and titles. It forces me to distill the book down into overarching themes and feelings instead of getting caught up in details. Thinking this way can help reorient and guide me on where to go with the manuscript.

For me, the manuscript, blurb (which is like a quick introduction to the book), and title all develop all together, instead of one at a time, going back and forth between the three pieces.

As a reminder, this beginning stages of making a book are the hardest and most frustrating parts. Get through these first few steps of planning and writing, and then you're in production mode. It's the creation part, the *pulling something out of nothing* that's so hard. At first you have no idea what that something is. You have to just keep your hands moving, and keep making, and then eventually, like a magician, something brand new will appear.

Believe in yourself, your ideas, and your book. You can do it!

Elements of a Successful Title

As you begin to think about the title of your book, here are some general guidelines to help you craft a title that captures the essence of your book.

Your book title should be relatively short (or easily shortened) so it will be easy to remember. It should be fun to say. Try using some of the poetry techniques (Refer back to Chapter 7). It should be original, as in there should not already be another book with the same title. Try searching your title idea on the internet to see what comes up. It should somewhat allude to the core idea of your book. You want it to give the reader an idea of what the book is about. It should set the tone of the overall book. Is this a funny book? Bedtime book? Silly book? Your title should reflect that. It should be easy to pronounce. You want people (especially a child) to be able to say it without much trouble. It could be a line from your book, your character's name, or a more abstract word or phrase that represents the book.

Example of a Great Title

One of my favorite picture book titles is "The Adventure of Beekle: The Unimaginary Friend" by Dan Santat. In conversation, most people shorten this title and simply call the book "Beekle". So the title is long, but it can be easily shortened. The made-up word, Beekle, is very original and quirky, which makes the title memorable (and easily found on the internet!). The longer title lets us assume the story will be about an imaginary friend named Beekle but makes us wonder what an "unimaginary" friend is. The made-up words and the phrase "adventures of" tell us this will be a slightly silly, imaginative, upbeat, and exciting story.

Writing a Blurb

A blurb is a summary of the book that's printed on the back cover or inside flap and also included on the sales page wherever the book is sold online. Writing the blurb before the book is complete encourages you to zoom out and remember the core of your book.. It helps guide the story and keep it on track.

We Are Fungi: book blurb

Here's the blurb on the back cover of my book, *We Are Fungi:*

> *"A picture book for kids ages 4-8. Enter our world. The world of fungi. The most mysterious and misunderstood kingdom on the planet. We are not plants. We are not animals. So what are we? From Veiled Ladies to Bleeding Teeth, learn how we eat, live, and control a part of the world you rarely even notice. Peek beneath the crispy leaves, peer inside your old lunch box, and poke between your smelly toes...We're here, we're growing, and even when you think you can't see us, we can always see you."*

CHAPTER 10

MAKING A WRITER'S DUMMY

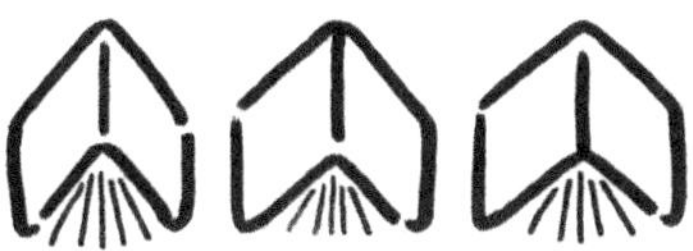

What's a Writer's Dummy?

A dummy is a small mock-up book made from folded paper. Usually, book dummies are made towards the end of the book making process and includes your final manuscript, sample spreads of final art, and refined sketches of all other spreads. This is what you submit to agents or publishers as an author/illustrator (More on all that in Chapter 19).

But making a dummy early in the process, with just your written story is a fantastic exercise that can help take your manuscript to the next level. This is a good thing to try after you've written at least a few versions and revisions of your manuscript. Making the dummy won't help you write better sentences or plotlines, but it can help you refine the pacing and see how your page turns work (or don't).

The dummy also gives you the experience of reading your story as a book, instead of just a flat piece of paper or computer screen. This can help you reorganize based on how the book reads (it's different than reading a 2-page manuscript!) and often reveals if you have too much text on each spread or in the whole book.

The point is: you should give it a try with your manuscript!

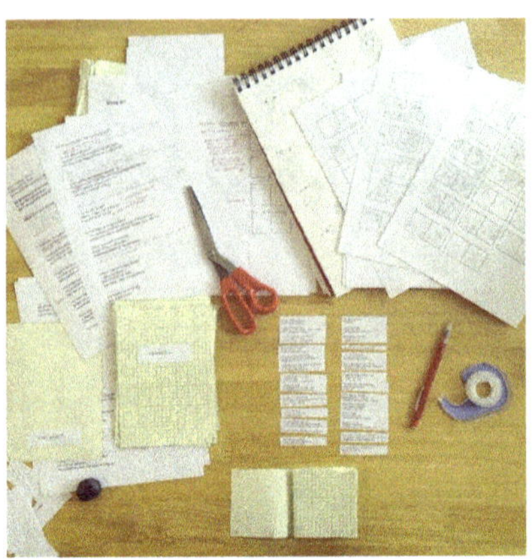

How to Make a Writer's Dummy

1. Cut out 8 strips of paper about the size of a dollar bill.
2. Fold the pieces in half and nest them together—now you've got a booklet with 16 spreads and 32 pages.
3. Label your front matter on the first couple pages, or however you've designed it: half-title, copyright, dedication, etc.
4. Print out your manuscript (tiny!) and cut out each paragraph, stanza, or sentence, based on what will go on each page.
5. Lightly tape the paragraphs onto the appropriate pages.
6. You may need to do some rearranging to figure out how to break up or pace the story, but that's what the dummy is for!
7. Once you think it's ok, it's time to analyze it!

Analyzing Your Writer's Dummy

Read through your dummy out loud and consider the following:

Do you have leftover pages that weren't used?
Maybe you need to consider spacing out your text more.

Do you have a lot of text on each page or many pages?
Maybe you need to cut words out of your manuscript or break up the text more. Try moving some paragraphs to other pages.

Does the reader know what the story is about within the first three pages not including the front matter?
You need to get to the story quickly! The action should begin by page 3. If your book dummy doesn't do that, try reorganizing or cutting from your manuscript and read through it again to see how it feels.

Is there tension in the story that makes you want to turn the page?
When you read the last sentence on a page, the reader should want to turn the page. It's overkill to have a cliff hanger on every single page, but it's good to have some sort of motivation or encouragement to turn the page. How can you add more tension or curiosity at your page turns?

Does your climax happen too early or late in the book?
Notice when the peak of your action happens. Is the resolution on the second to last or last spread? Try rearranging the climax and resolution and see how it feels when you read through again.

Do you have a good last line on page 32?
The last line is perhaps the hardest line to write. Or is it the first? Don't worry, that's what we're going to cover next!

CHAPTER 11

THE FIRST PAGE

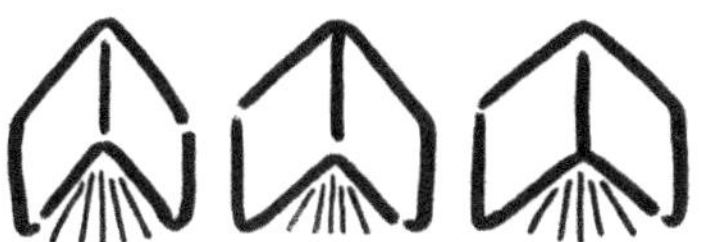

The Purpose of The First Page

I can't decide if I think the first page (and therefore the first line) of a story is the most important, or if the last page (and therefore the last line) is. Both carry heavy weights, both have near infinite possibilities, and both are extremely hard to write.

So now that you've written lots of versions of your manuscript (you should have at least 5 revisions by now) and have refined the order and pacing of your story with your writer's dummy, let's focus on writing (or rewriting) that formidable first line.

First Page Guidelines

The first page (and/or the first few lines) in your story should make a few things clear immediately.

- Who is the main character?
- What do they want? (ie. what is the conflict?)
- What is the setting?
- What kind of story is this?
- Why should I keep reading?

Example of a Successful First Page

Sounds like too much for one page to accomplish? Let's look at an example of a lovely opening page, from the book, *Don't Let Pigeon Drive the Bus* by Mo Willems.

> *"Hi! I'm the bus driver. Listen, I've got to leave for a little while, so can you watch things for me until I get back? Thanks. Oh, and remember: Don't Let Pigeon Drive the Bus!"*

Now let's compare this opening page to our guidelines from above.

Do we know who the main character is?
The bus driver is the first to speak, but I'd guess that Pigeon is the main character, since the bus driver is also leaving the story on the first page.

What does the main character want?
Pigeon wants to drive the bus, of course.

What is the setting?
This one is a little tricky. This book really has no setting, it's just a pigeon, a driver, and a bus on a solid color background. So, in that case, it does show us the setting, or at least tells us the setting is unimportant to the story.

What kind of story is this going to be?

The casual conversational dialogue implies a quirky, fun story. Also it's talking about a pigeon driving a bus right out of the gate, so we can expect it to be funny as well.

Does it hook the reader?

Yes! The thought of a pigeon driving a bus is absurd, so why would the driver ask us to watch his bus and then give us such a weird warning? The first page makes us want to find out why the pigeon shouldn't drive the bus, if the pigeon will drive the bus, and *how* the pigeon will drive the bus. It makes us want to turn the page!

All in all, a highly successful first page of a picture book, don't you think? Mo Willems knows what he's doing. But I'd be willing to bet he had to write lots and lots of quite terrible first pages before he came up with this brilliant one.

So get to it!

CHAPTER 12

THE LAST PAGE

The Purpose of the Last Page

So you've got a decent first page and opening lines of your story now, huh? Well, how does it end? How are you going to wrap everything up in a tidy little one-liner that makes the reader immediately smile or laugh or weep? How are you going to write an ending that is satisfying and believable, but not predictable?

Before we get into the nitty-gritty, here's a tip: your ending does not have to wrap up every loose end, answer every question, or resolve every plot point. It's ok to leave some mystery. In fact, your story will be more powerful and leave more of a lasting imprint on your reader if you *don't* reveal everything.

This goes back to our chat about the purpose of a picture book: you don't need to spell out your message to the reader on the last page. Leave some room for the reader to insert themselves into the story and interpret it in their own way. Give them the dots you think are important, and then let *the reader* connect them.

Ending Guidelines

Here are some questions to ask yourself about the ending of your story as you work on refining it. Depending on where your resolution ends, these could apply to the last page or the last 2-3 pages of your story. Often the resolution occurs on pages 30-31 and the wrap-up is on page 32.

- Is your ending predictable?
- Does it solve the problem/conflict posed in the beginning?
- Is the main character the one who solved the problem or resolved the conflict?
- Did your main character go through a transformation or change to get to this ending?
- Does the ending seem a little too convenient? Was the main character given the easy way out?
- Does the ending blatantly state a message? Remember, you should leave it up to the reader to interpret the message.
- And is the reader left with something? What does the reader feel at the end? Do they feel anything at all?

Example of a Successful Ending

There's a lot of pressure on the last page of a picture book, I know. So before you go swinging around in the dark, let's look at an example of a wonderful ending from the book, *Where the Wild Things Are* by Maurice Sendak. After visiting the island of Wild Things, Max said goodbye, got in his boat and sailed for what felt like years:

> *"and into the night of his very own room,*
> *where he found his supper waiting for him.*
> *And it was still hot."*

As a note, the first sentence ("and into the night...") is on the second-to-last page, and the last line ("and it was still hot") is on the last page of the book. Now let's compare this story ending to our guidelines from above.

Is the ending predictable?
No. We may have expected Max to come home, but I don't think many expected him to come home to his still warm supper.

Is the conflict overcome or the problem solved?
Yes, Max wants to be a wild thing, and he allows himself to feel his emotions and experience his inner wild thing.

Did the main character solve the problem?
Yes, Max came to his realizations on his own.

Is the main character transformed?
Yes, by becoming a true wild thing, he learns how to stand up to and master his inner wild thing (ie inner turmoil).

Is the ending convenient?
No. He has to sail for what feels to him like years to return to his home/reality.

Is there a blatant message?
No. There is definitely a message, but it doesn't state on the last page: "And then Max came home and was no longer angry at his mom and his mom was also not angry because she is still his mom and loves him no matter what he does." Wouldn't that be boring? Wouldn't it be better for you, the reader, to fill in the gaps with your own struggles with emotions and inner turmoil?

Is the reader left with something?
Yes, the reader feels Max's emotions of relief, love, and comfort.

It's a tall order to create a story ending that can do all that. Try refining your own ending with these questions and see what happens!

CHAPTER 13

REFINING A WEAK MANUSCRIPT

If you've been working on your manuscript, but it still feels like it's not quite there, or is weak is certain spots, here are a few tips and techniques to try.

Make your main character face three obstacles instead of just one.

The repetition of three obstacles or attempts to solve a problem is extremely common in stories, especially picture books. If your manuscript currently has your main character facing their conflict once or twice, try adding in another final attempt to find the solution. Usually, the three obstacles are related, or even just variations of the same obstacle. Experiment with breaking your conflict out into three separate obstacles and see how that feels.

Make sure your action is dependent on prior action.

One action or plot point should clearly lead to the next. One obstacle or attempt should build on the previous actions and decisions. This also means you don't want to have coincidences popping up that appear random or "too good to be true". The story should follow cause and effect. Think through: why is this plot point happening, what caused it to happen? If you can't answer that question, you may need to add in prior action or detail.

Escalate your plot in order.

Whatever number of obstacles or action plot points you have, be sure your character tackles them in order from easiest to hardest or least exciting to most exciting. The hardest obstacle with the most tension or drama will then be your climax.

Increase the suspense.

If your manuscript feels flat, try adding extra tension by making the reader worry if the character will overcome the obstacles. How you break up your action and page turns can especially help with this. You have to entice the reader to keep reading by hooking them into the story, which often happens a page-turn. Try out one of these techniques at a page turn and see how it feels:

- Ask a question
- Unfinished sentence
- Show extra tension
- Begin a confrontation
- Introduce excitement

Avoid writing visual descriptions.

Another technique that can help strengthen your manuscript is to avoid writing visual descriptions. As the writer, you should focus on crafting the action and dialogue. The visual descriptions should be communicated by the illustrator.

For example, you don't need to write that your character is wearing a red dress unless that fact is vital to the story for some reason. Things like clothing and most physical features will be shown in the illustrations and don't need to be repeated in the words.

If you are the writer and the illustrator, it's still good to avoid writing the visual descriptions. You can focus on the visuals once you begin drawing. Let the words do what they do best and the pictures do what they do best.

If you are not the illustrator, trust in your (future) illustrator to use their creativity to best create the visuals characters and story. Making a picture book with two people is a partnership, and the illustrator needs room to imagine with their own vision too!

Don't write summaries (show, don't tell).

Descriptive language is tricky. We're writing a picture book, not a novel, so we have to be careful with word count. Another tip for strengthening your writing is: Don't write a summary of a scene, write the scene! For example:

Instead of: "Max was bored."
Try: "Max flopped down on the couch and stared at the ceiling."

Both sentences communicate boredom, but the second option is stronger because it *shows* what the character does rather than *tells* a statement of a feeling. This way of writing involves the reader and forces them to interact with and think about the story more. The reader has to interpret what is shown and come to their own conclusion that Max is bored. This exchange between writer and reader makes a story much more powerful.

Both options could work in different situations. But in general, a solid rule in writing is to show, not tell.

Reduce your word count.

This can be one of the quickest ways to improve your manuscript. Your manuscript should be between 0–700 words. Each writer/editor/art director has their own preference, but less than 700 is standard. Writing a picture book is similar to writing poetry—you want to use just the words you need and no more.

It's natural to overwrite your first drafts. As you refine your manuscript, you can cut out what's unnecessary or redundant. The more you write, the better you'll get at editing and writing with brevity. Here are some techniques to reduce your word count.

Delete Descriptions

We talked about this earlier, but deleting descriptions is a great way to lower your word count. Remember, most descriptions will be shown in the pictures, so you don't need to waste precious words on them!

Delete adjectives

Adjectives are words that describe the qualities of nouns. Words like big, funny, green, or boring. Sometimes adjectives are good and strengthen the story, but sometimes they are unnecessary. Look at the adjectives in your manuscript and see if there are any that do not add much value to the story. For example:

Instead of: The ***tall*** girl fed the cat.
Try: The girl fed the cat.

Is the girl's height related to the action of feeding a cat? Or somehow relevant and important to the story? The illustrator can show that the girl is tall, so most likely, the word "tall" is unnecessary in this sentence. That's one less word in your manuscript! One word may not seem like much, but if you apply this and other techniques throughout your manuscript, they begin to add up!

Not all adjectives should be removed, but try to think about which ones are strengthening your writing and which may be weakening the writing. Each word should hold value and carry its weight!

Delete adverbs

Adverbs are words that modify (describe) a verb, adjective, or sentence. Adverbs often end in -ly. They include words like badly, warmly, or hastily.

Instead of: He ate his food ***quickly***.
Try: He gobbled his food.

Rather than writing a verb (ate) and adverb (quickly), you can communicate the same thing by writing a more specific verb (gobbled). This is a more specific and stronger word, and also allows you to delete another word from your manuscript!

Use the active (not passive) voice

Active and passive voice are two different grammatical voices. In the active voice, the subject is performing an action. In the passive voice, the action's target is the focus on the sentence. The subject is now being acted on by the verb, meaning the subject is passive. This makes more sense when we look at an example:

> **Instead of:** The cake is being eaten by the boy. *(passive)*
> **Try:** The boy eats the cake. *(active)*

In the example of active voice above, the boy (the subject), is performing the action (eat), on the target of the action (the cake).
In the example of passive voice above, the target of the action (the cake) is the focus on the sentence. The subject becomes passive. Instead of acting, the subject is now being acted upon by the verb. Writing in this way, in the passive voice, makes the sentence longer, indirect, and cumbersome. Writing in the active voice is much more direct, clear, and concise.

Go through your manuscript, go through and see if you used the passive voice anywhere. Try rewriting those sentences in active voice, and you'll probably be able to cut out a few more words!

Delete qualifying words

Qualifying words are words that are added to another word to its meaning, either by limiting or enhancing it. Qualifying words affect the level of certainty in a sentence. Some qualifying words include really, very, almost, just, somewhat, sometimes, usually, and most. Here are a few examples of qualifying words:

> **Instead of:** She was very interested in lizards.
> **Try:** She was obsessed with lizards.

Instead of: Her hair looked very nice.
Try: Her hair looked exquisite.

Instead of: He was feeling sort of worried.
Try: He was anxious.

Sometimes qualifying words are necessary, but often they make the writing sound hesitant, doubtful, or lazy. Try replacing qualifying words with more a more descriptive or confident word choice.

Delete extra words

There are some words that we all use in conversation and casual writing, but when writing a picture book, these words just take up unnecessary space! Try deleting these words from your manuscript:

There were, there was, it was

Instead of: *There was* a girl twirling on the table.
Try: A girl twirled on the table.

He saw, he looked, he heard

Instead of: *Sarah heard* her parents shouting in the kitchen.
Try: Sarah's parents shouted in the kitchen.

Which was, which is

Instead of: The plane, *which was* powerful, took off.
Try: The powerful plane took off.

Who was, who is

Instead of: The dog, *who was* well-trained, pointed at the cat.
Try: The well-trained dog pointed at the cat.

Skip unimportant parts story

If something is unimportant, get rid of it! For example, if it isn't important how the student got to school, you don't have to write about it. You only have so many words to use, so choose wisely!

CHAPTER 14

CHARACTER DESIGN (DRAWING)

In Chapter 8, we talked about character design from the writing perspective. If you plan on writing and illustrating your book, now is a good time to start thinking about character design from the illustration perspective.

Similarly to the writing side, good character design is all about making a unique, well-rounded, believable character. It's not just about what color hair they have or whether they wear it down or in braids. We're talking full character development here. So let's look at how to communicate a character's personality through how you design and draw them.

3 Criteria for a Successful Character

1. Particularities

As an illustrator, you are developing a whole little person with quirks, flaws, and personality. You need to show their personality by how they're drawn: what their proportions are, what they wear, how they smile, how they walk... everything!

A good exercise is to ask yourself: What makes this girl/boy/animal different? How is this a unique character we care about and not just another generic girl/boy/animal?

Particularities also make your character unique so they can be identified by the reader immediately. This could be anything from a hairstyle like a short bob or a particular accessory like a red striped shirt. But your choices here shouldn't be random—they should be conscious decisions. What does a short bob say about personality?

These little particularities can be obvious, like giving your character messy hair to show their wild nature. But they can also be more subtle, and it's often these subtle touches that instill personality and realism into your characters. Likely, your reader will not consciously think, "oh, this character has messy hair, they must be a little wild". But our eyes are trained to soak in details like that, and readers will absorb it, even if they don't totally realize it.

So remember, don't rely on the words to **say** your character is timid or messy or shy or outgoing—**SHOW IT!**

2. Possibilities

Your character should also have many possibilities, meaning they should be able to express a variety of emotions and poses and perform in any necessary situation in your story. For example: You may not want your character to wear a hat that covers their eyes—that would make their range of expressions much more limited and difficult to show.

You should also keep in mind, when designing your character, that you're going to be drawing this character over and over. That doesn't mean you should necessarily draw a simple character to make life easy for you, but you do need to be able to recreate this same character recognizably and consistently throughout the book.

For example, if your main character is a dragon think about how you will draw his scales. Is it feasible or necessary to draw every single scale on his body every time? Maybe it is! Or maybe there is another way to visually represent the scales that would be a tad simpler? There's no right answer, and everyone will draw a dragon in their own way with their own preferred level of detail. It's just worth keeping in mind that you need to be able to keep the character consistent throughout the book.

3. *Appealing*

A character doesn't have to be likable to be a great character, but they do need to be appealing. A main character can begin the story unlikeable, but they should be fairly likable by the end of the story, even if it takes the whole story to show a transformation that makes them likable. This way, the reader cares what happens to them in the end.

Not every character has to be likable though. Consider Cruella DeVille. You aren't supposed to *like* her, but she's an amazing character! Appealing means your character should be realistic, original, and flawed. No one is perfect, and no one wants to read about a perfect character. It would be boring and no one can relate to perfection. So your character needs flaws, just like a real person.

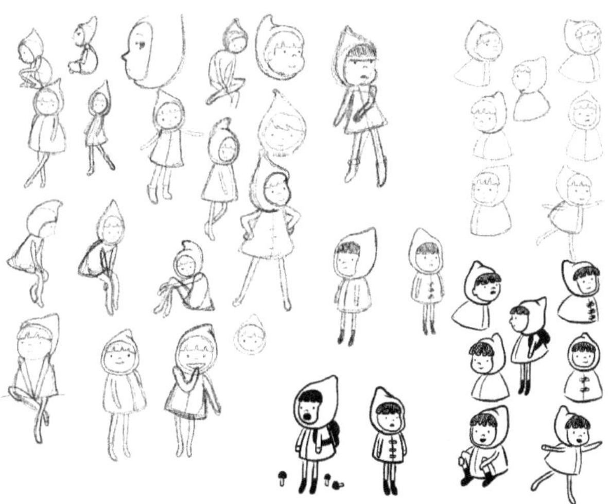

Elements of Character Design

Body Proportions

A character's proportions can communicate a lot right away about who they are and certain stories call for certain proportions. A more serious story might call for more realistic proportions, while a quirky story can utilize more offbeat proportions like large heads and big eyes. Younger characters typically have larger heads and larger eyes that are lower on their face. Older characters typically have smaller heads and smaller eyes that are higher on their face. These are just generalities though—not rules. Forget 'em and ignore 'em if you want!

Clothing

Just like with real people, how a character is dressed can quickly communicate a lot about their personality and identity. Clothing choice is a form of expression for all of us, and what you wear says something about who you are or how you're feeling that day. It's no different for your characters! What your character wears can easily tell the reader if your character is messy or tidy, eccentric or trendy, just to name a few!

Expressive Emotions

A character's face is often the best tool for displaying emotion. No person or character expresses the same emotion in the same way. When looking at your characters think about some of these aspects in terms of emotions:

- How big is their mouth? Do they have a big, toothy smile or a small smirk?
- Where are their eyes? How big are they? Do they usually keep them open wide, curious and excited? Or do they keep them half-closed, cool and relaxed? What about eyebrows?

Poses and Movement

In a picture book, it's usually not that imperative to draw your characters completely anatomically correct, but you do want them to be recognizable and believable. So try to make your poses somewhat based on reality, even if your character proportions are not. Focus on the gesture of the pose, instead of getting all the body parts correct. Exaggerating the pose a bit will also help to bring more emotion and excitement into the drawing.

Sub-Characters

Sub-characters can add interest to your story, as well as a secondary mini-narrative that is only in the pictures and not in the words. This also gives the child a special narrative that they can follow on their own before learning to read words.

For example, there is a mouse character (with his own little story) in every scene of the book, *Goodnight Gorilla,* but he is never mentioned in the words of the story. My daughter loves to follow along with the mouse's part in the story through the pictures and point him out on each page.

You can see more of my character design drawings for *We Are Fungi* on this book's Resources webpage found at the back of this book. For more specific drawing techniques and more on drawing in your own artistic style, see my book, *Sketchbook to Style: Discovering Your Style in Your Sketchbook.*

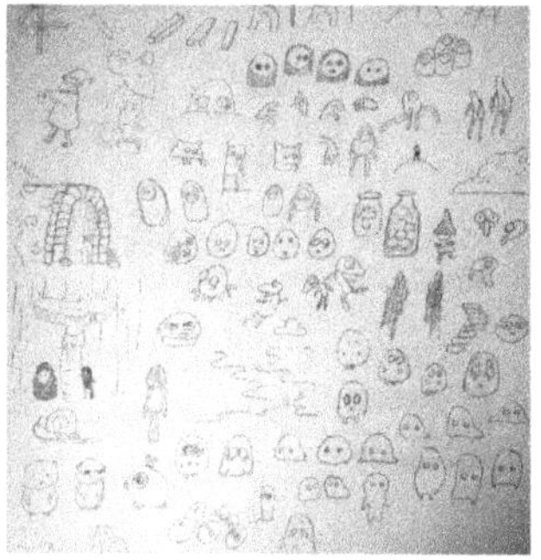

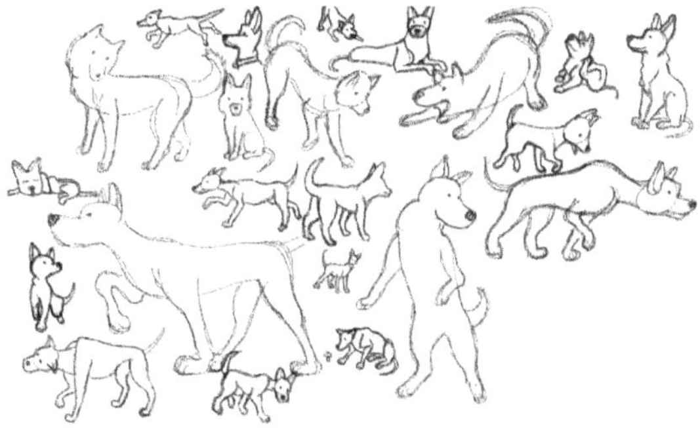

CHAPTER 15

TYPES OF PB ILLUSTRATIONS

Not every illustration in a picture book is a full-spread piece of artwork. Utilizing a variety of sizes and types of illustrations is key to creating a quality picture book. Mixing it up sets the pace of your book, creates rhythm, and allows your art and text to breathe.

So let's look at the different types of illustrations commonly used in picture books!

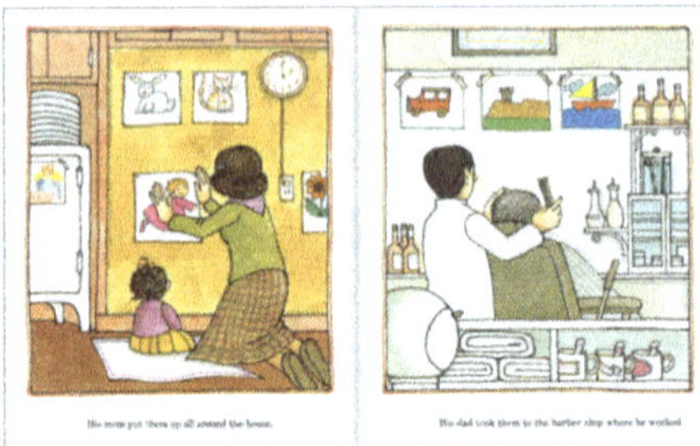

Boxed Illustrations

Ex: *The Art Lesson*
by Tomie dePaola

Boxed illustrations have defined edges, often a border or frame, and do not extend to the edges of the page. Not all boxed illustrations are fully contained within their borders though. Rules can always be broken!

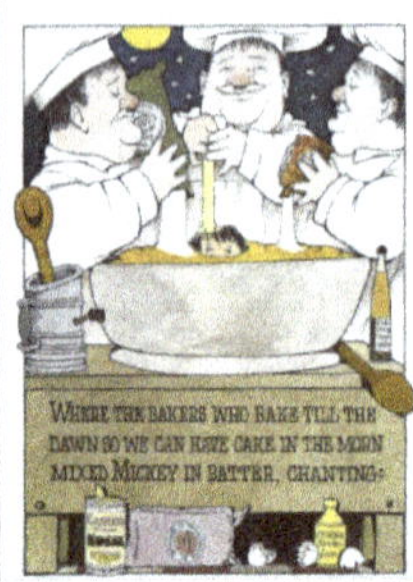

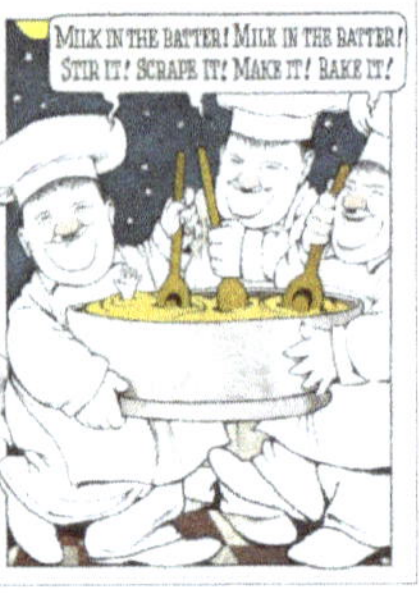

Ex: *In the Night Kitchen*
by Maurice Sendak

Here, you can see elements of the artwork breaking out of the box. A foot, a hat, a spoon, a speech bubble.

This is still technically a boxed illustration because it doesn't bleed to the edge of the page and has a border, but Sendak made the decision to cross some elements over the border, creating more depth and dimension. Both are successful in their own way!

Vignettes

Ex: *The Tale of Peter Rabbit*
by Beatrix Potter

Vignettes have edges that fade into the white space of the page. There is no defined edge or border. Beatrix Potter is a master of vignettes, and she uses their soft nature fantastically in all her books.

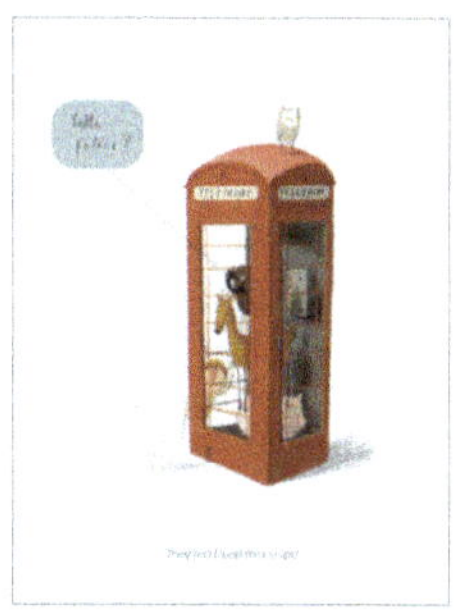

Spot Illustrations

Ex: *The Great Paper Caper*
by Oliver Jeffers

A spot illustration is a small free-floating illustration. It differs from a vignette because it usually has no background.

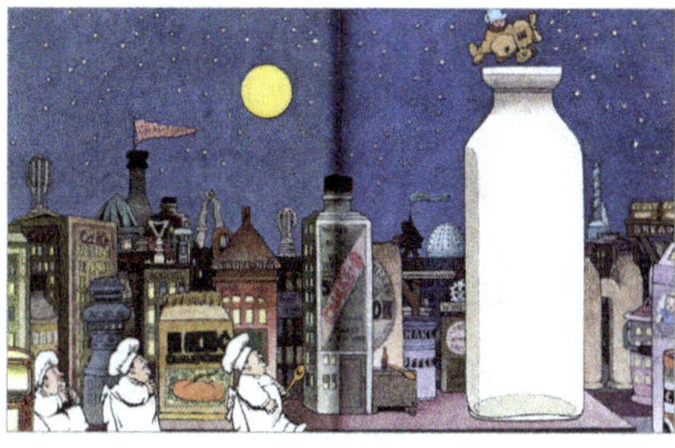

Full-Bleed

Ex: *In the Night Kitchen*
by Maurice Sendak

Full-bleed illustrations run off the edges of the page. These illustrations can be full-bleed across one page or across the entire spread. Full-bleed spreads are often used to heighten drama and are frequently used at the climax of the story.

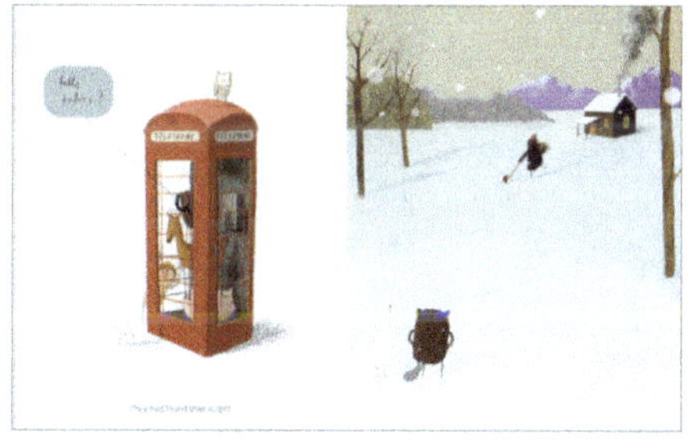

Combinations

Utilizing and combining the different types of illustrations adds interest and rhythm to your story.

Here is the full spread from *The Great Paper Caper* by Oliver Jeffers that we looked at earlier. Jeffers placed his spot illustration opposite a full-bleed page illustration. The two work together to move the story, time, and the reader's eye along.

CHAPTER 16

DRAWING A STORYBOARD

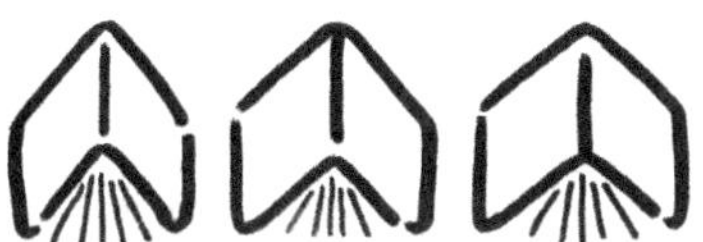

What's a Storyboard?

A storyboard is a visual thumbnail layout of your entire book. It's a tool to help you think through and plan your book. Storyboarding is a process of trial and error, and you'll need to make many different storyboards to see what works. Creating a storyboard allows you to:

- See how the story will progress
- See the book as a whole
- Create a rhythm with your pictures
- Focus on overall design and composition instead of details
- Create movement from page to page and spread to spread
- Balance busy and quiet pictures
- Balance types of illustrations
- See repetition and similarities

How to Storyboard Your Book

You can find and use my storyboard templates in the back of this book. There are three basic page layout options: landscape, portrait, or square. The page layout choice is up to you, and it's worth experimenting with different ones. You can always change this later on if you change your mind.

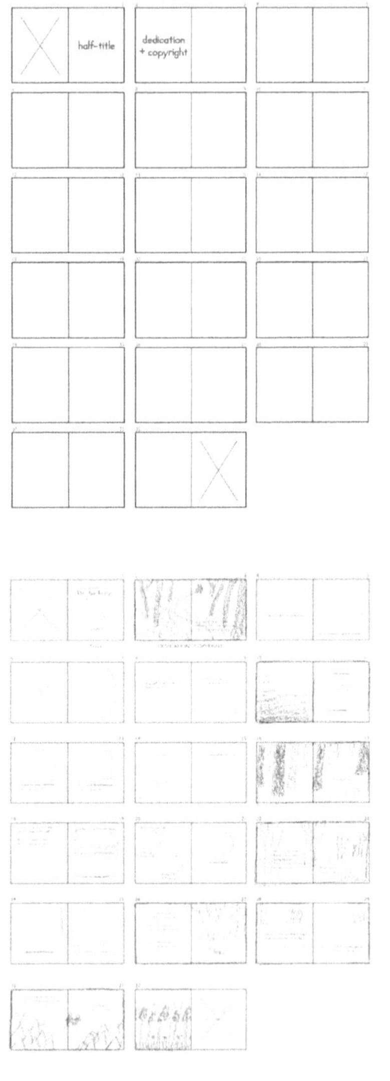

1. Block Off the Front Matter

The first 1–4 pages in a picture book are usually reserved for front matter (half-title, publisher, copyright, and dedication). So block off the first few pages for now and begin drawing your story on pages 3, 4, or 5. You can always change this in a future storyboard once you start moving things around.

2. Lay Out the Visual Story

Our initial goal is to lock in which parts of the story go on each page and decide what to draw and what *not* to draw. Don't try to draw nice, pretty pictures right now, just sketch rough shapes, and don't get bogged down with details.

Choose what to draw

On each page, what you *don't* draw is just as important as what you *do* draw. You have to choose what is most important. Remember: if the picture can say it all, then no words are needed, and vice versa!

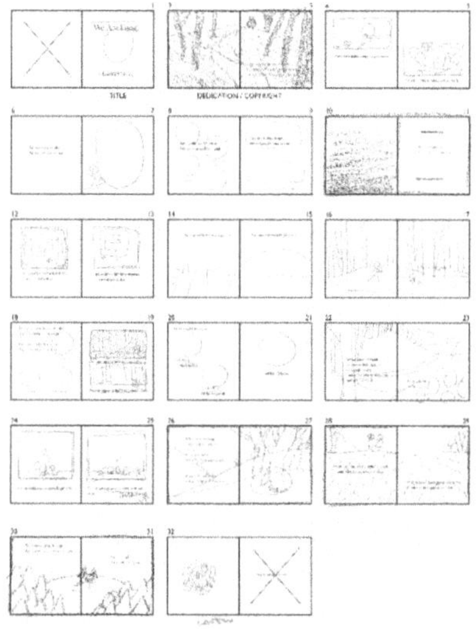

3. *Refine Composition*

Once you've gotten your story broken up, you can begin to refine your spreads.

Composition

Consider how you are using full bleed, vignettes, and spot illustrations. Do you need more illustration types? Refer back to Chapter 15. Consider the text and how it is incorporated into the composition.

Rhythm

A good exercise to refine your rhythm is to redraw your storyboard with only the large elements. This lets you concentrate on the overall design and composition, rather than characters and details.

Rhythm and pacing is often determined by the size of the pictures, so look at your use of vignettes, spots, or full-bleed illustrations. Imagine each illustration is a beat. You need to space them out so they flow together in harmony.

Viewpoint

When drawing, it can be helpful to think of each spread as a movie frame you're viewing through a camera lens. Should you be looking down on the character? Up at them? Close up? Far away? Viewpoints can communicate emotion and drama quickly.

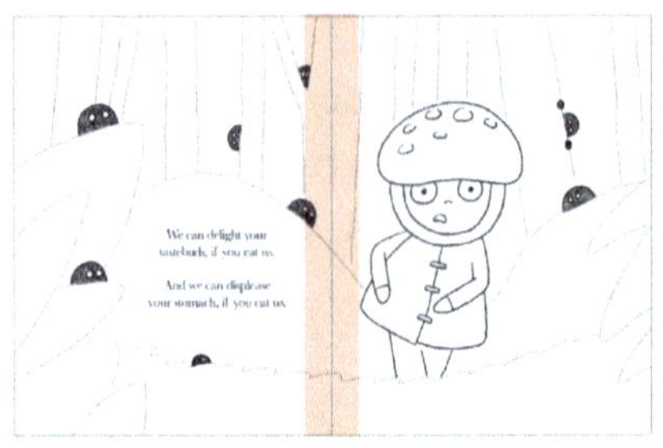

Gutter

Remember to be aware of the gutter on each spread as you draw. You don't want to place important elements in the gutter of the page, because a little bit of each page will be sucked into the spine and not visible once the book is bound. You can certainly have full-spread illustrations that cross the gutter—just avoid putting your main character's face or important action in the gutter.

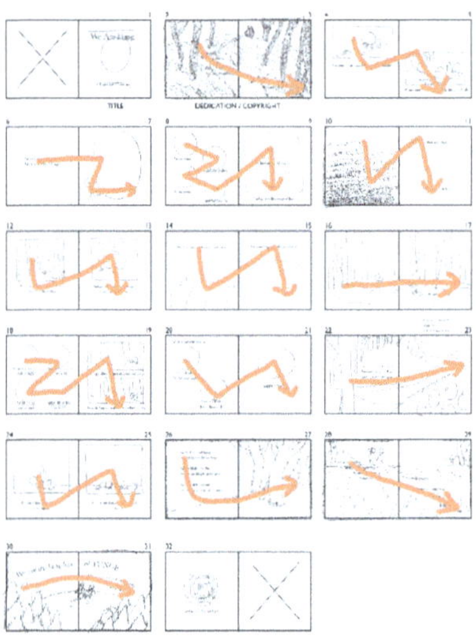

4. *Create Movement*

Now focus on the movement within pages and throughout the entire book as a whole. Here are some questions to ask yourself as you analyze your storyboard: Do your spread compositions pull your eye through the page, from left to right? Do the spreads look somewhat unified and flow together as a whole? Are your illustrations dynamic or static?

Movement and pacing help the story and characters feel alive, but they also move the story along and push the reader from page to page. Here are some ways to refine the movement in your book.

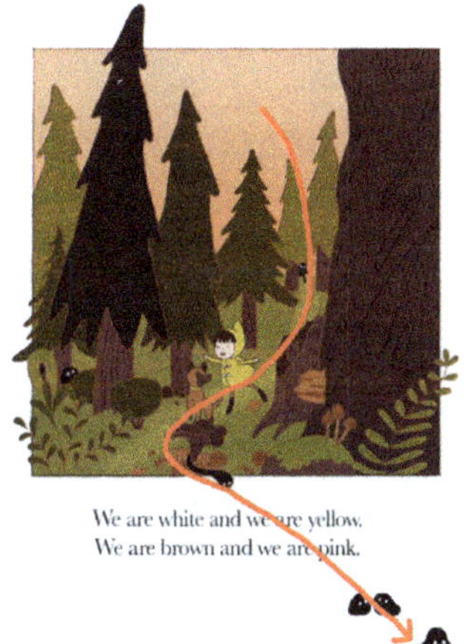

Movement in Page/Spread

The composition of each page and spread should create movement, pulling the reader from left to right, through the page, and to the next page. Individual elements in your drawings like setting or characters can also add movement. For example, your character could be leaping into the air, a hawk could be soaring through the sky, or rain could be falling slowly to the right. All of these things will create movement in your spread and make it more dynamic. Think about what lines of movement you've made.

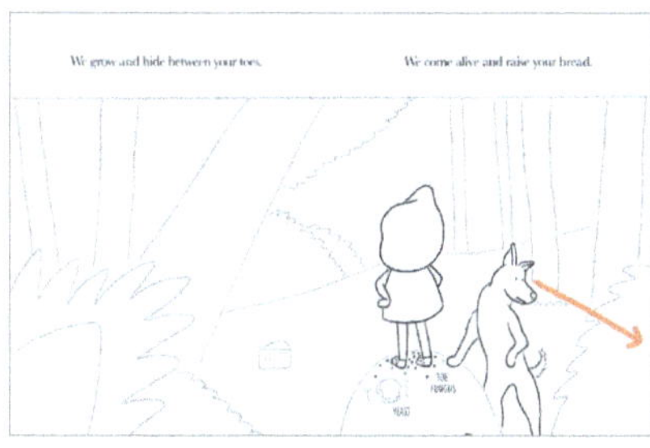

Movement in the Book (Page Turns)

Each spread needs to entice the reader to turn the page. Movement through the composition within a spread towards the bottom-right is one way to entice the reader, by leading the eye straight to the page corners (where they physically turn the page).

Another way to create strong page turns is by ending spreads with a moment of tension or uncertainty, so the reader is tempted to turn the page. For example, zoomed-in shots are often used at moments of high emotion or action such as elation or fear, and distant shots are often used during low points of emotion such as doubt or embarrassment.

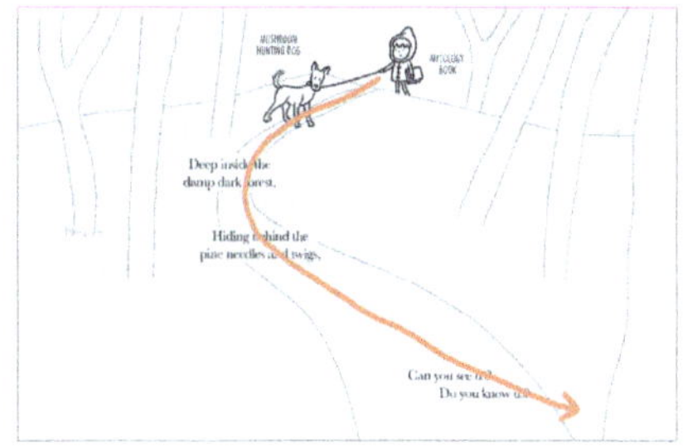

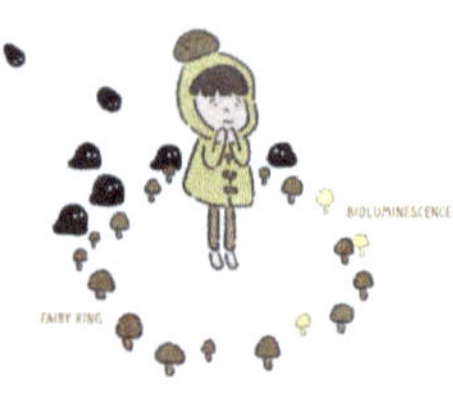

We glow green in the dark of night, and we commune in fairy rings.

Subplots

Integrating a subplot into your book is another way to create movement throughout your book. You can drop visual clues through the story to add extra meaning to the story, or even set up another visual narrative to run parallel with the main text. Clues like these entice the reader to turn the page to keep the story moving along and give the child a deeper interaction with the book, as they can read the secondary story on their own without words.

In my book, *We Are Fungi*, there is a substantial subplot of the girl being followed my little fungi creepies and the girl turning into a mushroom. Neither of these storylines is mentioned in the words, but they pull the reader along and can be read through the pictures.

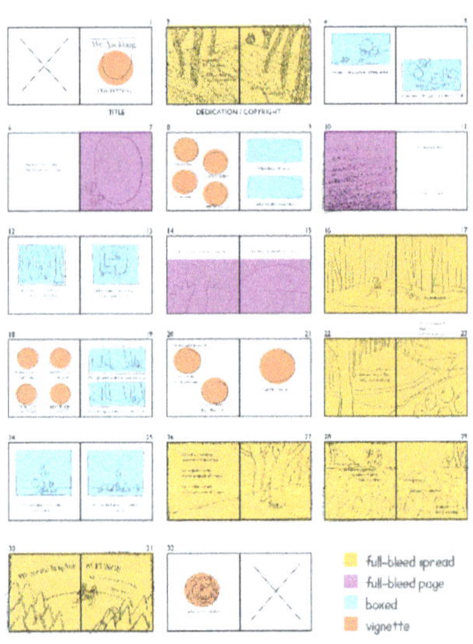

5. Analyze for Repetition

Just like in the text of the picture book, there should be a rhythm to your illustrations as well. Repetition of certain images or design layouts can help emphasize rhythm. This helps the reader follow and enjoy the story and makes the moments when you break from the repetition all the more powerful and exciting.

Ask yourself these questions about repetition in your storyboard:

- Is there repetition in your page compositions?
- Are there too many of the same types of illustration?
- Is there variety in how your characters are posed?

- Is there repetition and variety of viewpoints?
- Do you have a good balance between loud, busy images and quiet, still ones?

Continue drawing more and more variations of your storyboard if you find there is not enough or too much repetition of any elements.

Feeling stuck and confused?

If you're having a hard time with your storyboard, a helpful exercise is to storyboard an existing picture book. Choose a book you admire and redraw it as a storyboard. Go through it page by page, drawing a quick sketch of each spread on your storyboard template. Don't try to recreate the style or actual artwork. Focus on the shapes, illustration types, text placement, and general composition.

Think through these questions as you study the book:

- How many pages is it?
- How many words to they put on a page?
- What elements are in the front matter?
- On what page does the story begin?
- How many spreads for the story?
- Do any pictures get caught in the gutter?
- How do they combine illustration types?
- How do they inject movement in pages and spreads?
- How are the endpapers treated?

This exercise helps you see how an experienced illustrator uses a variety of compositions and repetition to create rhythm and pacing in their book. It's a great learning tool and taught me a lot about how to storyboard, so I recommend trying it out!

CHAPTER 17

REFINING A STORYBOARD

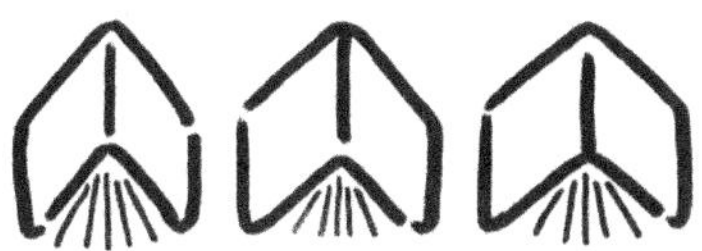

Now that you've got your story broken up into spreads, paced well, and the general composition and typography laid out, we can start refining and adding details. In the next few pages I'll share the three steps I took to refine my storyboard for *We Are Fungi*.

To see these images in larger and in color, visit the resources webpage for this book: *https://might-could.com/mcmb-resources/*

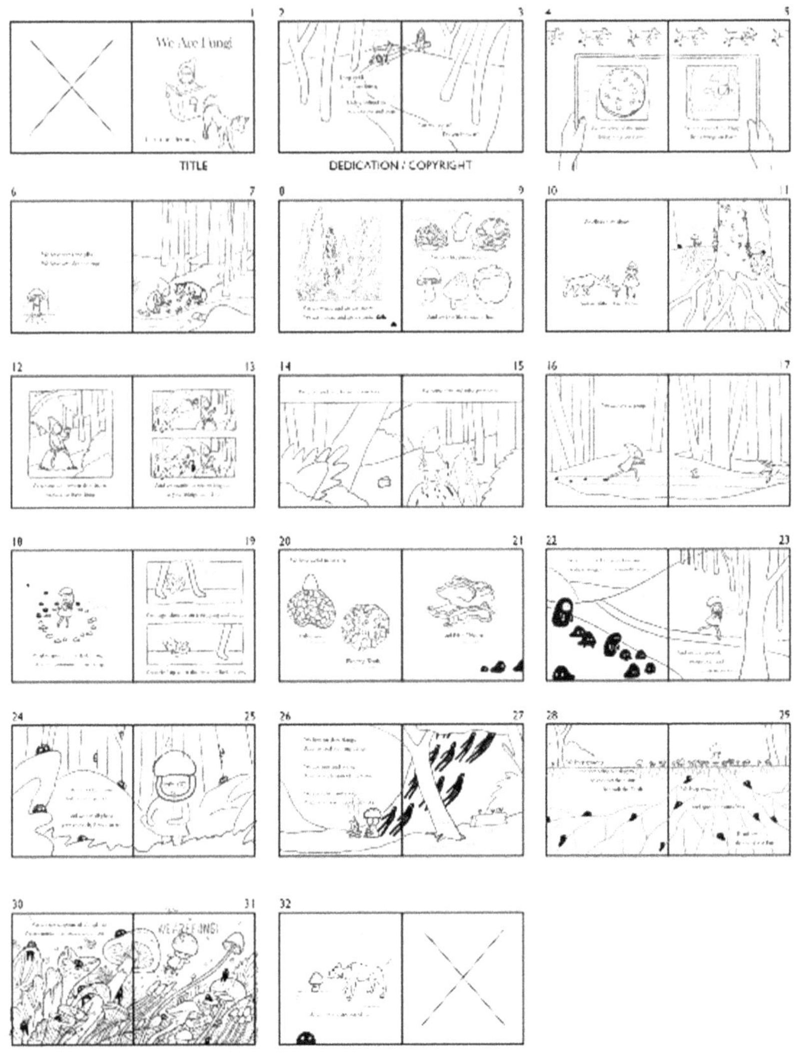
We Are Fungi
TITLE
DEDICATION / COPYRIGHT

1. Draw a more detailed storyboard.

It's time to finally start drawing our characters in the story and fleshing out the visual details! Our goal now is to redraw the storyboard with our character designs, drawing more refined illustrations than our loose sketches before.

At this stage, I like to draw digitally so I can zoom in and draw more details, while still using the storyboard format. I draw on my iPad with an Apple Pencil. If I'm just sketching (like here), I use the Procreate app directly on the iPad. As I get further in this process and need more digital tools (and a higher resolution with more layers), I use Photoshop on my computer and mirror the screen onto my iPad using Astropad.

You certainly don't have to do any of that though, and can choose to remain on paper! It's up to you and how you draw best.

As you draw, remember that this is still our storyboard. Try not to get swept up in one spread and take it too far. We want to balance working on all the spreads at the same speed so it all develops as a unified book. One exception to this could be the spread you think of as the climax of your book. It's reasonable to spend a little more time and detail getting that page where it needs to be, as it is one of the most important. In my storyboard to the left, the climax is on page 30-31, and you can see I drew a bit more detail there than in the other spreads.

Just like the other storyboarding steps, you'll most likely need to make multiple storyboards at this step until you're happy with it! Be patient and try not to rush through this stage—it's one of the most fun!

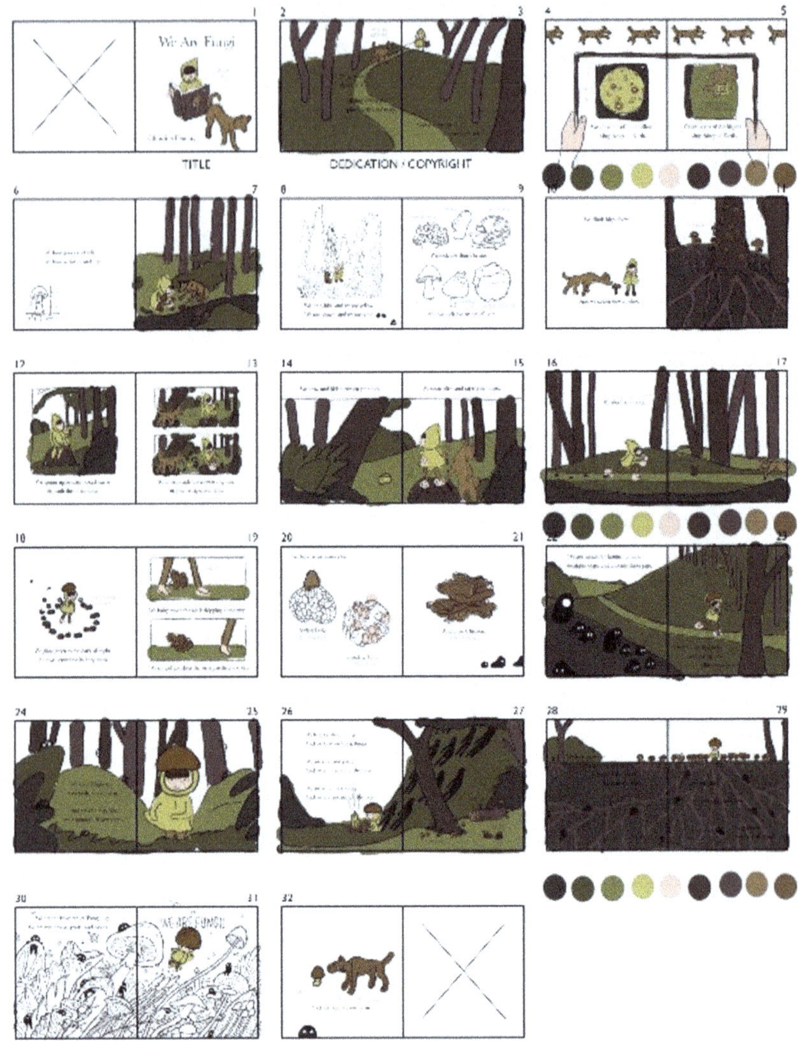
We Are Fungi
TITLE
DEDICATION / COPYRIGHT

2. Add color to your storyboard.

Once you're content with your refined sketches in the storyboard, you can begin adding in color. I like to do this digitally as well, so I can quickly edit and try out different colors.

To do that, I bring my storyboard into Photoshop or Procreate and loosely paint in colors. Sometimes the color palette works right away, and sometimes I need to fiddle with it a long time to get it to feel how I want it to.

Just as with our composition/design stage, we want to think about repetition and balance with color, using it to lead the eye and create unity throughout the book. That's why planning your colors in the storyboard stage is so helpful—it lets you quickly see how the colors are repeated throughout the whole book, creating a consistent, unified feel.

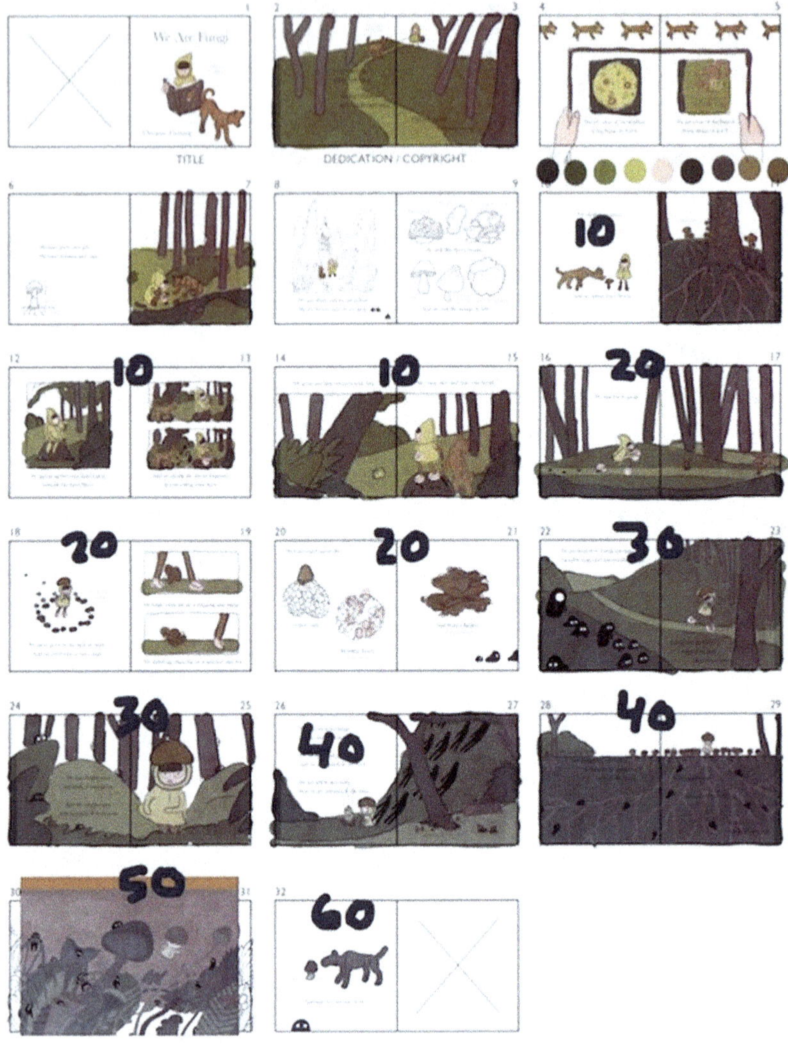
TITLE
DEDICATION / COPYRIGHT
10
10
10
20
20
20
30
30
40
40
50
60

3. Add any other details to finalize your storyboard.

You may be done with your storyboard after deciding on colors, or you may have other details you want to experiment with here in the storyboard stage before you move on.

For my book *We Are Fungi,* I wanted the color palette to shift over the course of the book, evoking the sun setting and night coming on. So in my storyboard, I played with some digital editing (hues, layer adjustments, textures, opacities, etc) until I captured the mood I was going for. (The numbers written on the storyboard are notes to myself about what opacity level I was using for adjustment layers.)

It's much easier to play with these things here in the storyboard than on separate spreads (and files) later on. You can always come back to this stage if necessary.

CHAPTER 18

CREATING SAMPLE SPREADS

Taking two spreads to final lets you explore and nail down the style of the book, without having to do the book over and over as you discover that style. Also, if you plan on submitting your book to publishers, this is part of what they want to see!

That's right, you don't have to illustrate the whole book before you submit it to publishers. Editors or agents just want to see a couple of examples of what the final art will look like to get the idea. If you submit an entirely completed book, it gives them the impression you think it's finished and perfect and that you won't be open to revisions, which is a major turnoff for them. I'll talk more about all that in Chapter 19.

When choosing the two spreads you're going to take to the final, try to choose two that will give the best impression of the entire book. This may mean you choose one spread from the beginning and one towards the end. Or one spread with spot illustrations and another with a full-spread illustration. Try to present a range!

How to Create a Sample Spread

This process will vary wildly depending on how you plan on illustrating your book. I'm going to show you my process of creating a final spread from my book, *We Are Fungi.* But please keep in mind that this is just an example and is only one way of illustrating—you can and *should* do this in your own way! There are endless possibilities and the choices are all up to you!

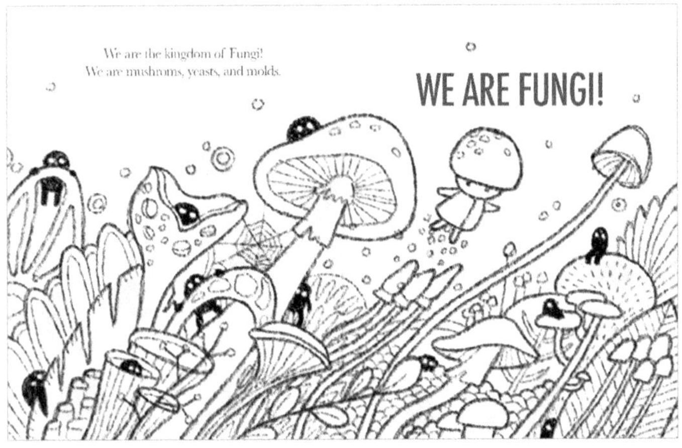

1. Blow Up the Sketch

First, I grabbed the sketch from my storyboard, opened it up as its own document in Procreate on my iPad, and blew it up to full size. This book was going to be 8 in x 10 in, so I blew my sketch up to a full-spread size adding in a 1/4 inch bleed: 16.25 in x 10.25 in at 300 dpi. Including bleed on your final artwork means your illustration will stretch beyond the final size of the book. When printed, the bleed will be cut off, but this bleeding past the edge ensures that the cut will be correct and not include any blank white paper. A 1/4 inch bleed is standard.

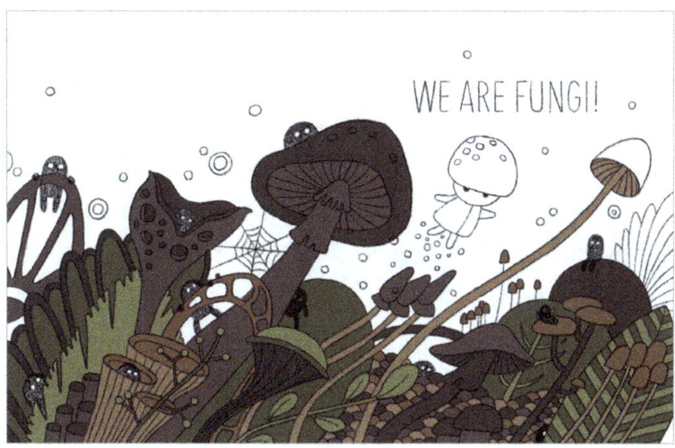

2. *Draw linework and color*

Next, I set the original sketch to a low opacity. On a new layer on top of the sketch, I drew out the "final" linework and color.

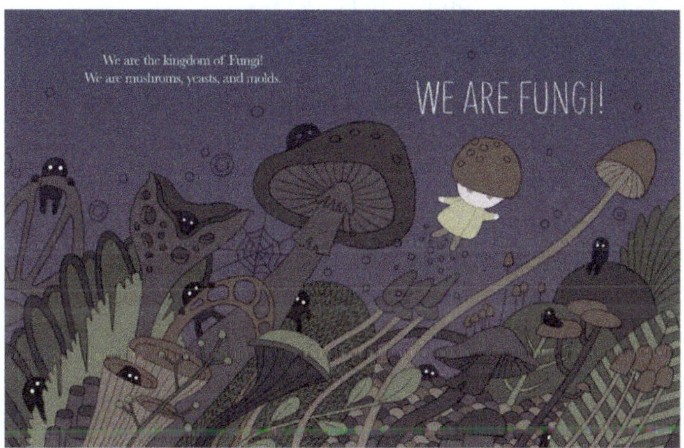

3. *Digital editing*

Then I exported that as a .PSD file and brought it into Photoshop for further digital editing. I played around with color, adjustment layers, and textures...

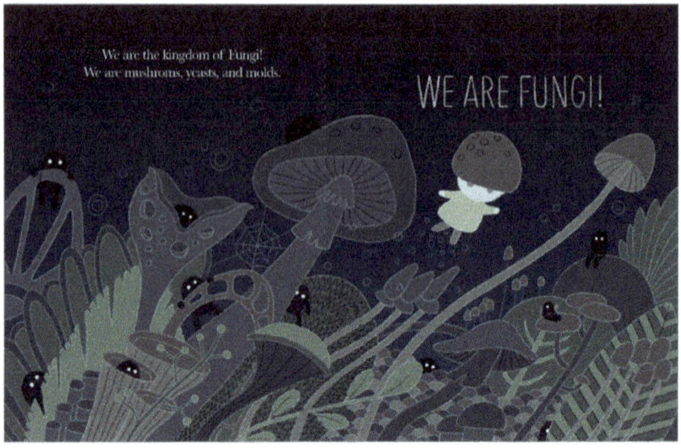

...until finally I got it right! But then I realized the all-digital production was a bit flat and didn't have the depth and organic feel I wanted. So I decided to pivot a bit and try creating many of the elements by hand with pen and ink (See? This is why we create sample spreads to find these things out early on!)

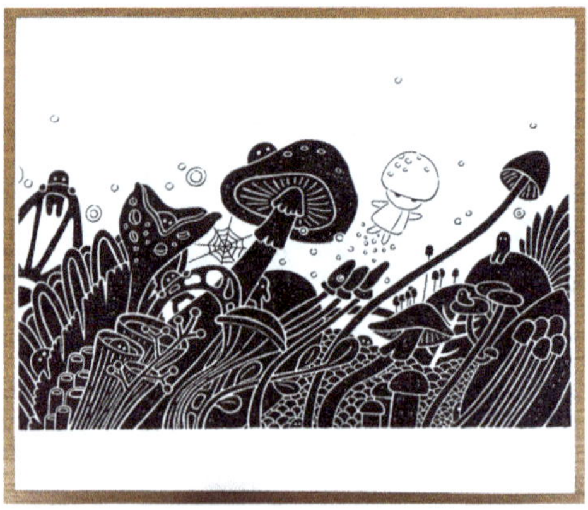

4. Hand-drawn textures

I printed out my linework and traced over it using a light table onto Bristol board paper with a Tombow Dual-Tip pen. Then I filled in the shapes with a loose pen texture that is a cornerstone of my personal style (and something I enjoy doing!)

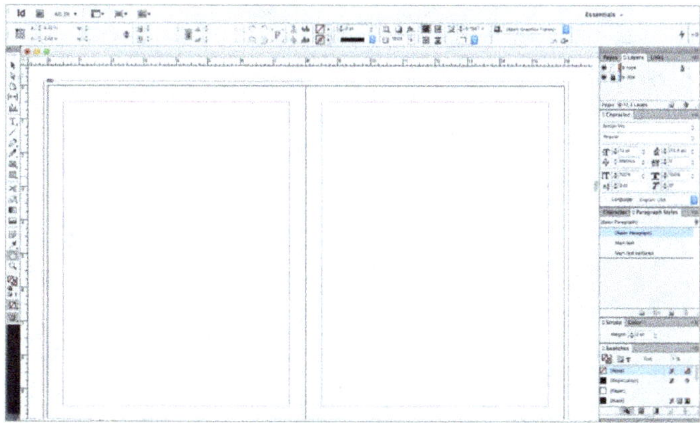

5. Final book design file

Then I created my design file for the whole book spread at the final size. The final artwork was created in Adobe Photoshop and I used Adobe inDesign to lay out the book.

Here are this book's InDesign file specifications:

- **Number of pages:** 42 (facing pages)
- **Each page:** 8 in x 10 in
- **Bleed:** 0.125 in
- **Top, Bottom, Outside margin:** 0.5 in
- **Inside margin:** 0.375 in
- **Gutter:** 0.125 in

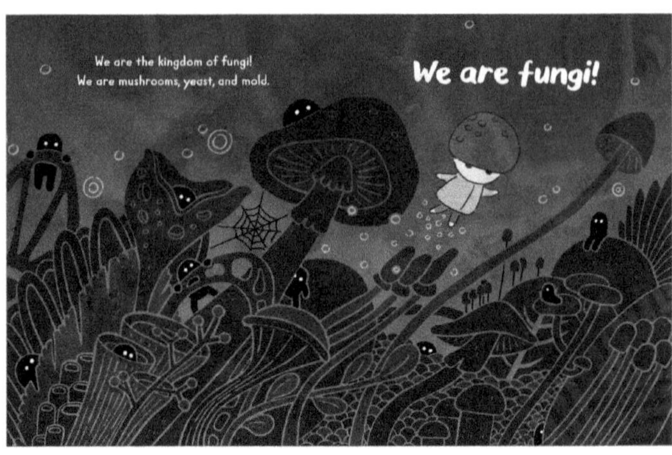

6. Place artwork + add typography

For this book, I used a custom font that I made previously based on my handwriting. I set the main text to font size 20pt over 34pt leading. But that's just what worked for this font and this book. It's hard to say what a common font size for a children's book is because every font is different.

Hooray! Now the sample spread is done!

I hope seeing this example helps you get started on your own sample spread. You definitely do not need to follow this as instructions. You should make your book in whatever way suits you and your art and your book best!

CHAPTER 19

SUBMITTING YOUR BOOK TO PUBLISHERS

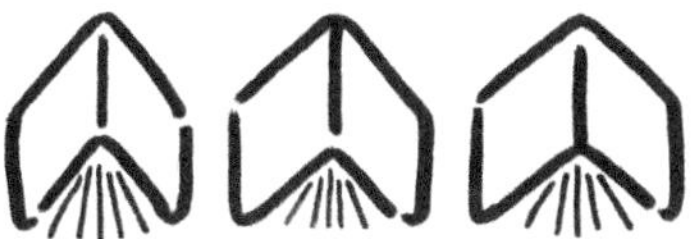

Before you even begin to *think* about submitting your book to publishers, it should have already gone through rounds and rounds of revision and be as close to golden as you can get it. Publishers get hundreds and thousands of submissions, so you need to make sure your book shines! Show your book with sample spreads to other artists or readers (and kids!) and see how they respond. Consider their feedback and make any changes you think would make your book stronger. Do the work!

If you think your book is ready, let's dive into the steps to submitting your book to traditional publishers! (Note: If you are not interested in traditional publishing and wish to self-publish instead, you can skip this chapter and move on to Chapter 20: Creating the Final Artwork.)

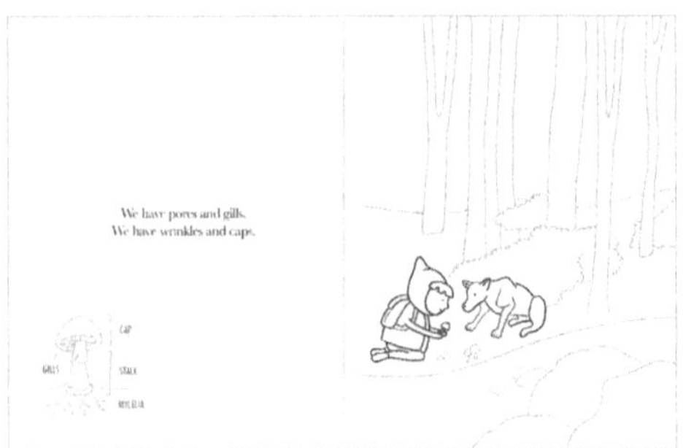

1. Make your book dummy

As I mentioned before, you shouldn't submit a fully finalized book to publishers. They want to see what's called a Book Dummy, which is a mock-up of what your final book would look like. If you are submitting to publishers digitally, this will be a PDF file. If you are attending a conference, you can bring your dummy as a printed booklet. Your book dummy should include:

- All 32 pages of your book, including front and back matter.
- 2-3 sample spreads in full color, showing how the final artwork will look (See Chapter 18).
- All other art should be drawn as refined sketches in grayscale. You can see an example of a refined sketch from my *We Are Fungi* book dummy above. How refined your make your sketches is up to you, but you want to make them clear enough that the publisher gets a good feel of the artwork.
- The book should be full-size (See Chapter 21 for more guidance on setting up your book design file).
- The text of your story should be typeset alongside the artwork. If you're not a designer, just do your best! Don't worry too much about the typography, the publishers will mostly be looking at your story, writing, and artwork.

You can see my full *We Are Fungi* book dummy as an example on the resources webpage found at the back of this book.

2. Research publishers

You shouldn't just blindly submit to any publisher you can find. Each imprint has its preferences, and many only publish certain types of books (ie. only novels or only non-fiction). So don't waste your time submitting to one who doesn't publish a book like yours.

Spend some time digging around on the internet to find out which publishers publish what. You can also go to the library or bookstore and look at the publisher info for picture books you think are similar in age, tone, or style to yours. There are many different types of publishers as well, including Traditional Trade, Mass Market, Small Press, and Educational. You'll need to decide which is right type of publisher is a good fit for your book.

The so-called "Big 5" publishers are Penguin Random House, Macmillan, Harper Collins, Hachette, and Simon & Schuster. Submissions to these publishers are highly competitive, but there are lots of smaller publishers too!

3. Make your submission list

Make a spreadsheet or list of the publishers you think would be interested in your book. When considering a publisher, be sure they are open to unsolicited submissions. Many publishers only accept submissions they have requested or submissions from agents.

Most editors at SCBWI (Society of Children's Books Writers & Illustrators) conferences will open up their submissions to attendees after the event. This allows you to submit where you wouldn't have regularly been able to and gives you the chance to make a face-to-face connection with the editor you're submitting to.

Many publishers prefer to be submitted to exclusively (meaning you only submit to one publisher at a time and don't submit to anyone else until you've received a reply from them). If you decide to submit exclusively, you should tell them so in your cover letter.

Common Question: Do I Need an Agent?

The short answer is that you don't *need* one, but many authors find it helpful to have one. An agent can submit to more places than you as just an author can, including the major publishers. Part of their job is to make connections with editors and art directors so they know what individual editors and publishers like, so they can send your manuscript to the right person. Having an agent also makes you more reputable, as their reputation reflects on you.

In exchange for all this, you will pay the agent ~15-20% of what you earn. However, you only pay the agent once you get a book deal. An agent should *never* ask you for money before you sign a deal with a publisher. They don't make money until you make money, and if they say otherwise, they are trying to take advantage of you and not behaving as a professional agent would.

Having an agent or not is a personal decision. Many authors have agents and many don't. If you decide to submit to agents, the process is very similar to submitting to publishers—research good fits, make a spreadsheet, and start emailing!

4. Follow submission guidelines

Above all else, follow the submission guidelines stated on the publisher's website. Almost all publishers accept submissions via email If you're emailing your submission, you can send a PDF of your dummy in spread format. Be sure to name the file with your name and your book title, such as: *Christine_Nishiyama_Title_Dummy.pdf*

Typically query letters (a letter to ask an editor if you can send them your manuscript), are generally not required for picture books. But check the publisher's guidelines and submit a query first if that's what they request. A query letter is very similar to a cover letter.

5. Write your cover letter

As part of your submission, most publishers expect to see a cover letter. Some people literally send a cover letter, but most treat their email as their cover letter. Keep your letter as brief as possible while still communicating everything you want to. Address your letter to a specific editor's name, not "To whom it may concern". And triple-check that you spelled their name right!

Your letter should be professional, but also friendly, and should match the voice and tone of your writing. You can organize your letter into three paragraphs: Intro, Story, and Bio.

The Intro paragraph should explain why you are submitting to this particular publisher/editor. Did they publish a book similar to yours? Name that book. Did you meet this editor at a conference? Remind them.

The Story paragraph should dive into describing your book. State the title of your story and include the estimated age group and type of picture book (board book, non-fiction, etc.) Explain why you're the best person to have written this book. Then pitch the story in a short two-sentence teaser. Don't explain the entire plot—excite them! Think of the pitch like a movie trailer.

The Bio paragraph should tell the editor a little about yourself. Keep the details professional. Don't list out superfluous information, but do include any expertise you have relevant to the topic. List any previously published work (no big deal if you don't have any). Include any pertinent degrees you may have like creative writing or something related to the subject of your book. If you don't have a relevant degree—don't worry! A degree is definitely not required or a deal breaker. You can also include any related professional organizations you belong to, like SCBWI (Society of Children's Book Writers and Illustrators).

Finally, wrap up and thank them for their time!

6. And then... wait.

Most publishers list a response time along with their submission guidelines on their website. For example: *If you don't hear back from us in 6 months, we have declined your manuscript.* If they don't list a response time, the standard is to wait three months before following up. You can then send a polite email asking about your submission.

I know, three months seems like forever and it's excruciating to wait! But that's just the way it is, unfortunately. The publishing industry moves slowly, and the process of an editor reading your manuscript, considering it, and possibly showing it to other co-workers, the marketing team, etc takes time. They also get a bazillion submissions a day, so it's a lot to handle. And that's on TOP of the editor working on their acquired in-progress books.

So give them time and try to be patient and optimistic!

7. Don't stop making books!

Book publishing is a tough business. The statistics are wild—some claim that for every 10,000 picture book submissions, 3 get published. All you can do is try to make the best books you can and don't give up!

A great piece of advice I've heard from many people over the years: Don't spend more time trying to get published than trying to become a better writer. Send out your story, kiss it for good luck, and instead of staring at your inbox for a year, start making your next book!

CHAPTER 20

CREATING THE FINAL ARTWORK

Working with a traditional publisher is no longer the only option for writers and illustrators. If you wish, you can choose to bypass that entire process and self-publish your book yourself!

That's not to say it's any easier. In fact, I think self-publishing is harder. If you don't have an editor, designer, or marketing team working with you, that means *you* have to do all that work yourself. Some find that liberating and exciting, and others find it unappealing or daunting. The choice is yours!

If you decide to self-publish, the next chapters will walk you through the remaining steps of creating your picture book. You may have more work to do as a self-publisher, but you also have complete control over how the book is made, as well as making your own deadlines and working at your own pace.

The first step is to create all the final artwork for your book!

This process is just like the process of creating the sample spreads, and will vary wildly depending on how you plan on illustrating your book. I'll show you another example from my book, *We Are Fungi* here, but again, this is just one way of doing it! You do you!

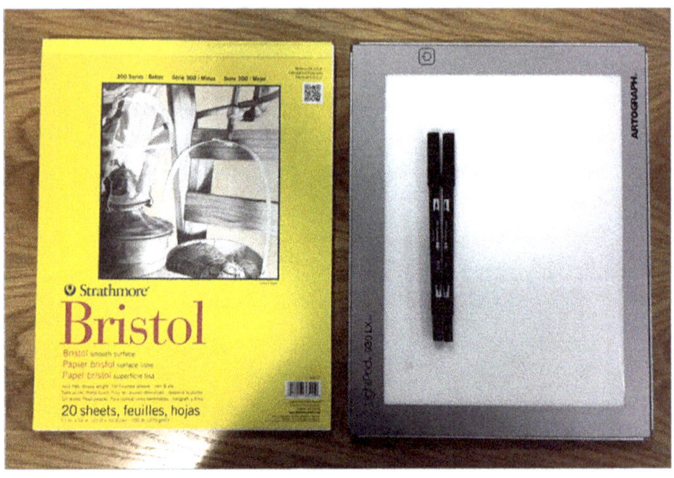

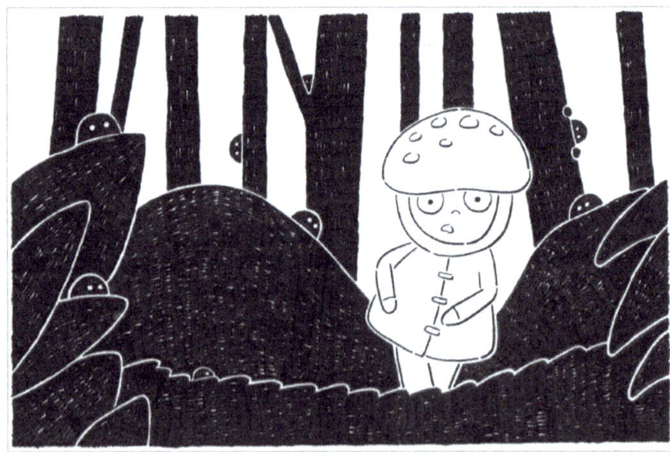

1. Draw the final art

For this book, I hand drew most of the artwork on Bristol board, using Tombow Dual-Brush pens. I blew up my refined sketch, printed it out, and placed it on a light pad so I could draw the finalized version on Bristol board on top.

I drew each spread as large as possible so the detail and texture would be rich. Each original artwork page was 11 in x 14 in. Some artists choose to draw at full size and some choose to draw bigger—it's up to you! Even drawing smaller can work as long as you're able to get it high-res enough to digitally blow it up to the full book size.

Then I took the drawings to a local printer and scanned them all at 600 dpi so I had them as digital files. (300 dpi would be fine, but I figured it's better to have 600 dpi if you have the option!)

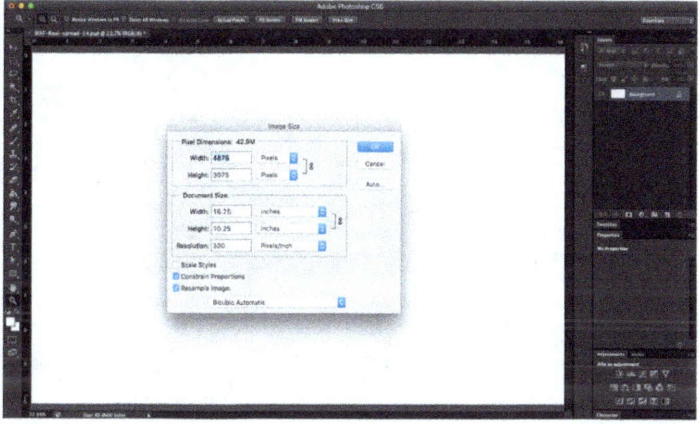

2. Open a new Photoshop file

Next, I created a new PS file with the dimensions of the final book with a .125 in bleed on each side. For this book, that ended up being 16.25 in x 10.25 in at 300 dpi.

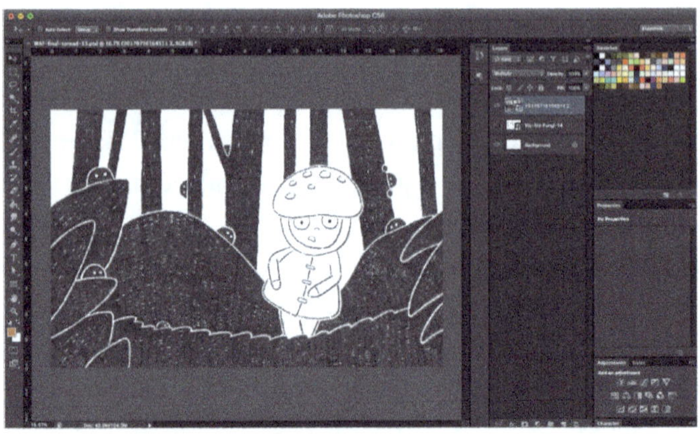

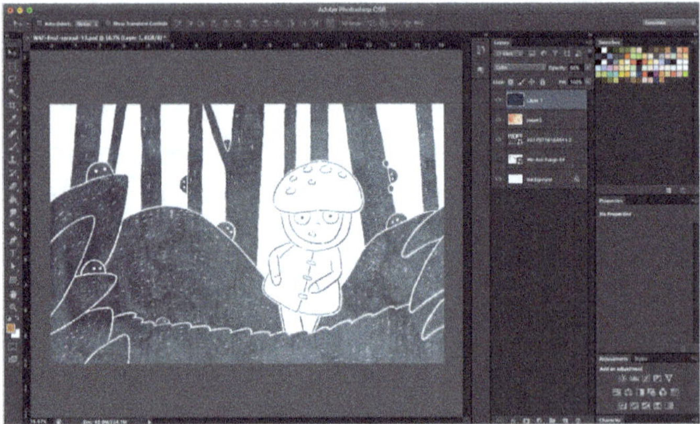

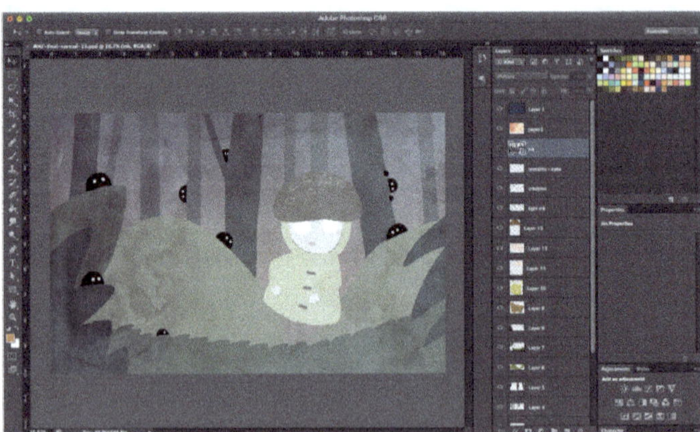

3. Digital editing in Photoshop

Then I placed my final artwork into Photoshop. From there it's a long process of trial and error, fiddling around with color, adjustment layers, and textures, and sometimes redrawing...until it feels good! This step takes the longest and is continuous experimentation. It's fun as long as you don't rush and remain open to the possibilities!

Here is the final artwork for this spread:

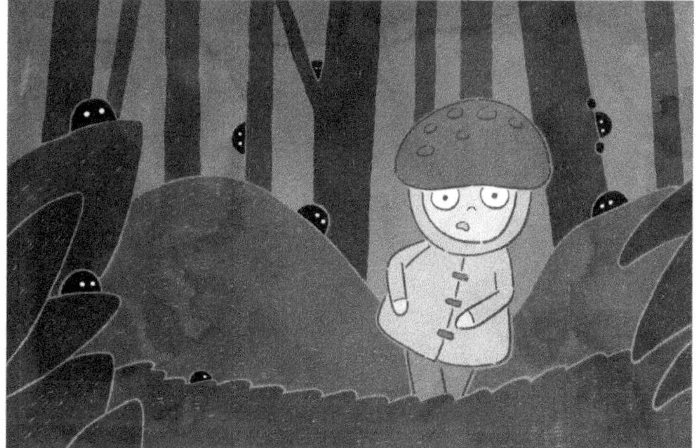

CHAPTER 21

CREATING THE BOOK DESIGN FILE

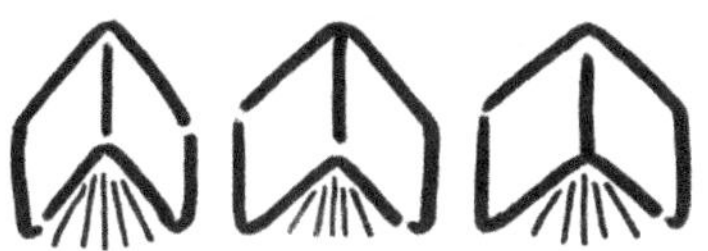

Book Design File Size

You'll need to compile your book in a design program, like InDesign or something similar. This file should be sized for printing and include margins, bleed, and gutter. Here are the InDesign file specifications for my book, *We Are Fungi*:

- **Number of pages:** 42 (facing pages)
- **Each page:** 8 in x 10 in
- **Bleed:** 0.125 in
- **Top, Bottom, Outside margin:** 0.5 in
- **Inside margin:** 0.375 in
- **Gutter:** 0.125 in

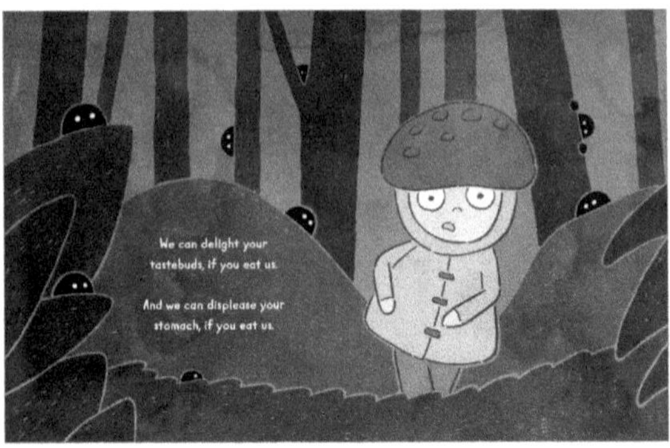

Typography

There aren't many standards for typography when it comes to picture books. It's hard to say what a common font size for a picture book is because it depends on the font. For this book, I used a custom font that I made previously based on my handwriting. I set the main text to font size 20pt over 34pt leading. Leading is the space between lines of text. Your type size may end up being very different!

One helpful exercise can be to take a photo of a published book and place that image into Photoshop, then try to type on top of it to see what size and leading they may have used. It's not super accurate, but it gives you a general idea of size and spacing.

You should also print out one or more of your final art spreads at full size to see how the typography size and space between lines looks and reads in real life. The screen can be deceptive!

Front Matter

Half Title

There are many ways to design a half-title page and some books don't have them at all. I like to design a simplified version of the cover for my half-title. You can see the half-title and copyright for *We Are Fungi* on the next pag

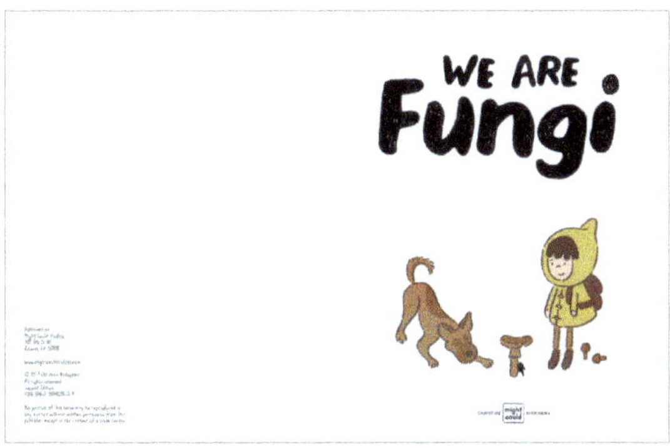

Copyright

The first or last page of your book should include the book's copyright and publishing information. Here is a template for copyright info that you are free to fill in and use for yourself!

> Published by Your Name (or Doing Business As Name)
> 123 Street Name City, State 12345
> www.yourwebsite.com
> © Year Your Name
> All rights reserved.
> First Edition
> ISBN #
> No portion of this book may be reproduced in any
> manner without written permission from the publisher
> except in the context of a book review.

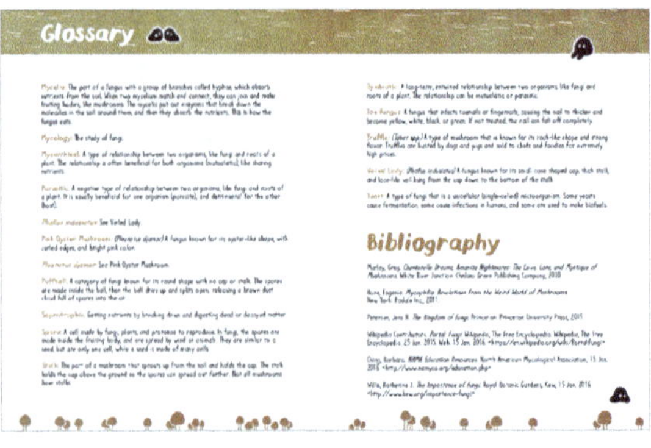

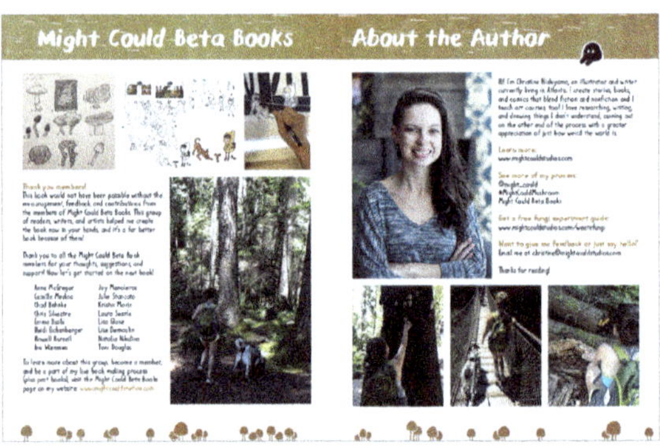

Back Matter

Not every picture book has back matter, but most non-fiction books do. *We Are Fungi* is (mostly) non-fiction, so I created a Glossary, Bibliography, About the Author, and a note about the group of artists that helped give me feedback. Be sure to have your website listed prominently so readers can easily find you and more of your books!

You could also choose to design end papers for your book, though this is more of a special design element and not as necessary for printing as it used to be. It is also usually not an option if you are doing print-on-demand.

CHAPTER 22

DESIGNING THE BOOK COVER

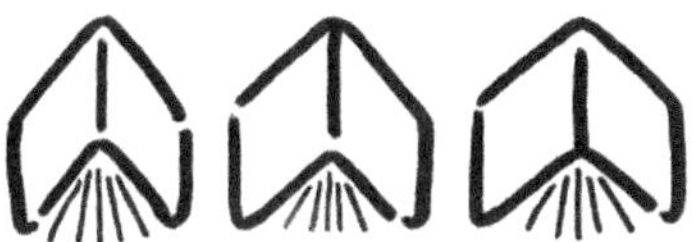

Your book's cover should give readers a good idea of what your book is all about at quick glance. What's the mood? Who are the main characters? What's the art style?

You don't need to include everything from your book. Think about what is most important to your story, or what makes it different from other books.

Also consider about how the book cover will look as a small thumbnail image on a webpage or how it might stand out on a bookshelf.

Look at some of your favorite books and see how they designed their covers. What elements did they choose to highlight? How did they treat the typography? Does the cover accurately represent the mood, colors, and characters from inside? How does the cover entice readers to pick up and read the book?

Elements on Front Cover

There are a few elements you should be sure to include on the front cover of your book. The book's title obviously, and the subtitle if you have one. The author and illustrator's (or author/illustrator's) name. Most covers include the main character, though some choose not to, if they have something more important to focus on.

If you are self-publishing, you may also choose to include a logo for yourself or your business/studio. You're technically a publisher now!

Elements on Back Cover

On the back cover, you can include more text and information about the book. You can include the blurb you wrote earlier, that serves as a brief description of the book. You can add your business name/logo again, and should also add your website. You can look at how publisher's usually do this on their own covers.

The other important thing about the back cover is to leave a blank space for the barcode. You'll need to look to your printer for more details on how to do this as each printer will have different specifications. They will most likely have downloadable print templates for different sizes of book's that will show you exactly where to place this blank barcode space. Then they will place the actual barcode for you.

Here are some examples of book covers from my books.

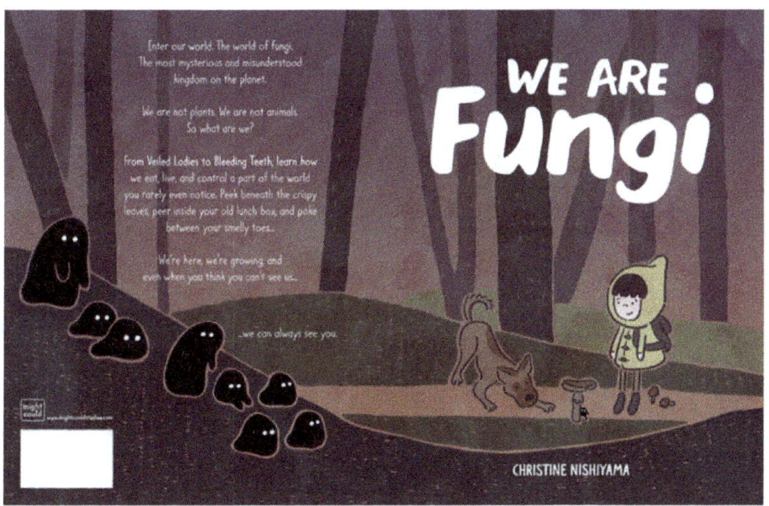
Enter our world. The world of fungi.
The most mysterious and misunderstood
kingdom on the planet.
We are not plants. We are not animals.
So what are we?
From Veiled Ladies to Bleeding Teeth, learn how
we eat, live, and control a part of the world
you rarely even notice. Peek beneath the crispy
leaves, peer inside your old lunch box, and poke
between your smelly toes...
We're here, we're growing, and
even when you think you can't see us...
...we can always see you.
WE ARE
Fungi
CHRISTINE NISHIYAMA

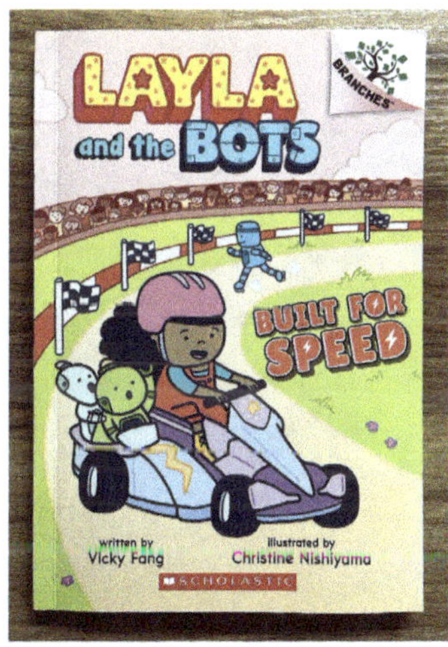
LAYLA
and the BOTS
BRANCHES
BUILT FOR SPEED
written by
Vicky Fang
illustrated by
Christine Nishiyama
SCHOLASTIC

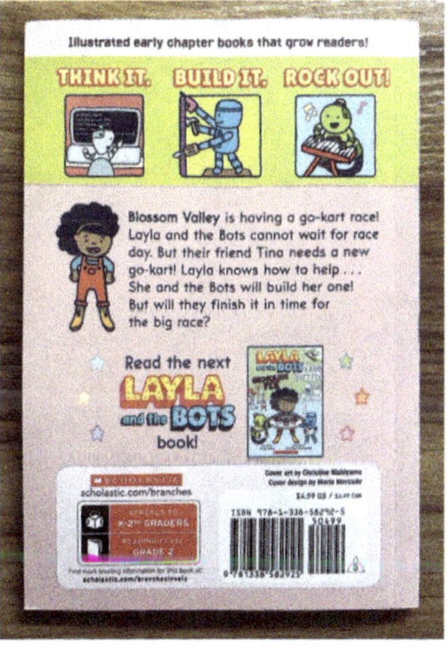
Illustrated early chapter books that grow readers!
THINK IT.
BUILD IT.
ROCK OUT!
Blossom Valley is having a go-kart race!
Layla and the Bots cannot wait for race
day. But their friend Tina needs a new
go-kart! Layla knows how to help . . .
She and the Bots will build her one!
But will they finish it in time for
the big race?
Read the next
LAYLA
and the BOTS
book!
scholastic.com/branches
K-2ND GRADERS
GRADE 2
ISBN 978-1-338-58292-5

CHAPTER 23

MARKETING YOUR BOOK

You may think you don't need to market your book until it's published, or that if you publish with a traditional publisher, you won't need to do any marketing work. Neither is true!

It's smart to start promoting your book before it's even finished, and definitely before it's published. And if you're working with a publisher you'll still be expected to promote your own book. The difference is if you self-publish, it's all up to you—there's no marketing team. While that means more work for you, it also means you get to decide how your book is promoted. You don't want to advertise on social media? Then don't! You want to give away some books for free? Then do that! You're the boss.

Personally, I'm an introvert and have a hard time asking for things, so marketing does not come easily to me. But over the years of being an indie artist, I've come to find my own way of doing it that feels good to me.

So don't worry if you're starting to squirm in your seat a little thinking about asking people to buy your book. Let's do it the non-spammy way, shall we?

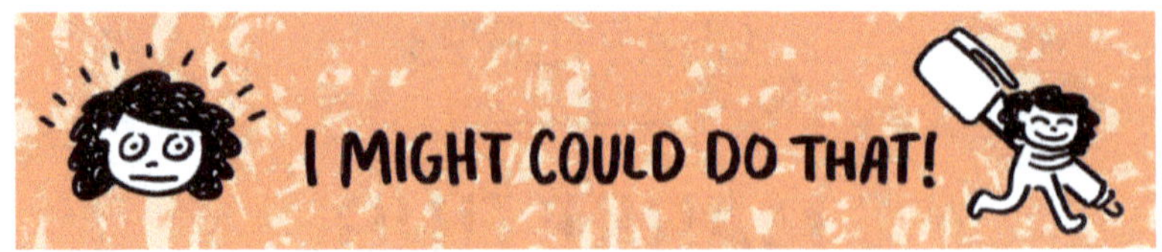

Email Newsletter

An email newsletter is the most direct way to communicate with potential readers and build an audience for your books. It's never too late to start an email list and over time, it will become your most valuable asset.

Email Platforms

I started by email newsletter in 2016 and have used MailChimp, ConvertKit, and am now using Substack. My newsletter has shifted over the years from monthly updates about classes and products, to personal essays and sharing my book process.

Substack is an amazing new option for email newsletters because it has a built-in network and is free! Other platforms like MailChimp and ConvertKit charge you per subscriber. Substack has less marketing tools like segmenting and funnels, so your choice depends on what you are trying to achieve with your newsletter.

For me, my substack, *I Might Could Do That*, is a place to share my work, connect personally with my audience, and build my audience. I tell my newsletter subscribers first about any new books, classes, or projects.

Sharing Your Process

My email newsletter is also where I share my book making process, which is one of my primary ways of promoting my book. See? Promotion can be as simple as sharing the work as you make it, and inviting others behind-the-scenes! Each time you share a process post, people are alerted and reminded that you have a new book coming out soon. And once the book is released, they'll be all the more interested and invested in the final product!

Start your email newsletter now if you don't have one and start experimenting! (See the Resources page at the back of this book if you'd like to join my newsletter.)

Email Launch Sequence

So you have an email newsletter and you're sharing something about your book as you make it, but what will you say when your book is out? How will you convince people to give it a chance? Here's a snapshot of the emails I sent out to launch *We Are Fungi*:

- **Email 1: Making Of**
    - I shared some behind-the-scenes process of how the book was made and announced the release date of the book. I sent something of this nature out about every other week throughout the entire time I was making the book.
- **Email 2: Book Trailer**
    - The day before book launch day (when the book is available for purchase) I sent an email with a link to the book trailer I made.
- **Email 3: Book Launch!**
    - I let them know the book was now available to purchase, linked them to my Sales Page, and asked them to buy, share, and review it. I also gave the ebook away for free to people who subscribed to my email list.
- **Email 4: Reviews/Response So Far**
    - A week after Book Launch, I thanked those who had bought the book, recapped some of the reviews that had come in, and asked again for people to check out the book and share it with their friends.

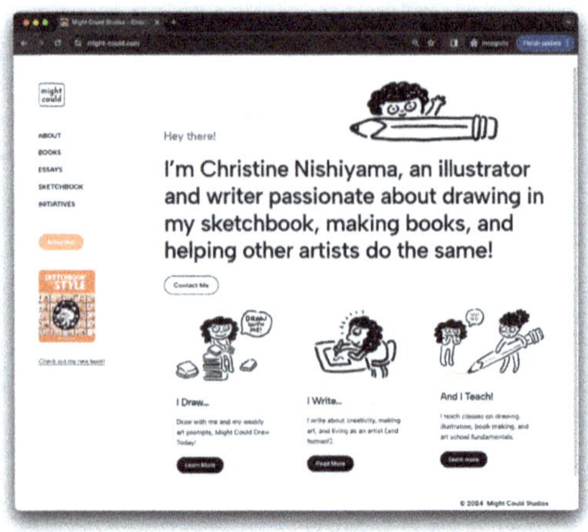
ABOUT
BOOKS
ESSAYS
SKETCHBOOK
INITIATIVES
Hey there!
I'm Christine Nishiyama, an illustrator and writer passionate about drawing in my sketchbook, making books, and helping other artists do the same!
Contact Me
I Draw...
Draw with me and my weekly art prompts, Might Could Draw Today!
I Write...
I write about creativity, making art, and living as an artist (and human!).
And I Teach!
I teach classes on drawing, illustration, book making, and art school fundamentals.
© 2024 Might Could Studios

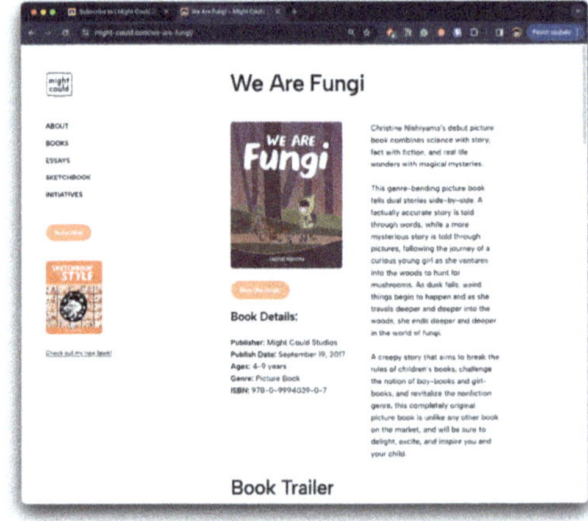
ABOUT
BOOKS
ESSAYS
SKETCHBOOK
INITIATIVES
We Are Fungi
WE ARE Fungi
Book Details:
Publisher: Might Could Studios
Publish Date: September 19, 2017
Ages: 4-9 years
Genre: Picture Book
ISBN: 978-0-9994039-0-7
Christine Nishiyama's debut picture book combines science with story, fact with fiction, and real life wonders with magical mysteries.
This genre-bending picture book tells dual stories side-by-side. A factually accurate story is told through words, while a more mysterious story is told through pictures, following the journey of a curious young girl as she ventures into the woods to hunt for mushrooms. As dusk falls, weird things begin to happen and as she travels deeper and deeper into the woods, she ends deeper and deeper in the world of fungi.
A creepy story that aims to break the rules of children's books, challenge the notion of boy-books and girl-books, and revitalize the nonfiction genre, this completely original picture book is unlike any other book on the market, and will be sure to delight, excite, and inspire you and your child.
Book Trailer

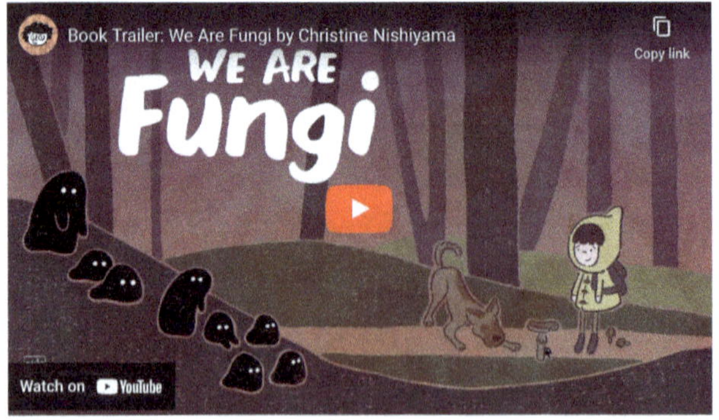
Book Trailer: We Are Fungi by Christine Nishiyama
Copy link
WE ARE Fungi
Watch on YouTube

Book Sales Page

If you don't already have a website, you should make one now. It can just one page with a photo, bio, and contact info if you want to keep it simple. You could also create a Portfolio page if you are an illustrator. I'm not going to go into a full web design tutorial here, but I use WordPress as my CMS to build the webpages, and Dreamhost to host my website. You can see the current home page of my website to the left and at: *https://might-could.com/*

Once you have a website, you can create a page on your website specifically for your new book. As an example, you can see a screenshot of my sales page for *We Are Fungi* to the left and the full page here: *https://might-could.com/we-are-fungi/*

Your sales page can be as simple or complex as you like. You could just include an image of the cover, the title, and a link to where they can buy the book. For my sales page, I included the cover image, blurb, reviews, book trailer, behind-the-scenes videos, and two activity sheets. Be sure to have an obvious button or link for them to go and buy the book at the top and bottom of the page! If you can, it's nice to include photos of the physical book once it's printed, and that can be updated after your printed proof comes in.

Book Trailer

I created a super simple book trailer to promote my book and sent it out to my email subscribers. I used iMovie to edit together the digital files of the book, zooming in on the artwork. I also recorded a friend's daughter reading the book blurb from the back cover and used that as audio for the trailer.

You can share your book trailer wherever you are sharing other promotional items. As an example, you can see my book trailer on this book's resources page: *https://might-could.com/mcmb-resources/*

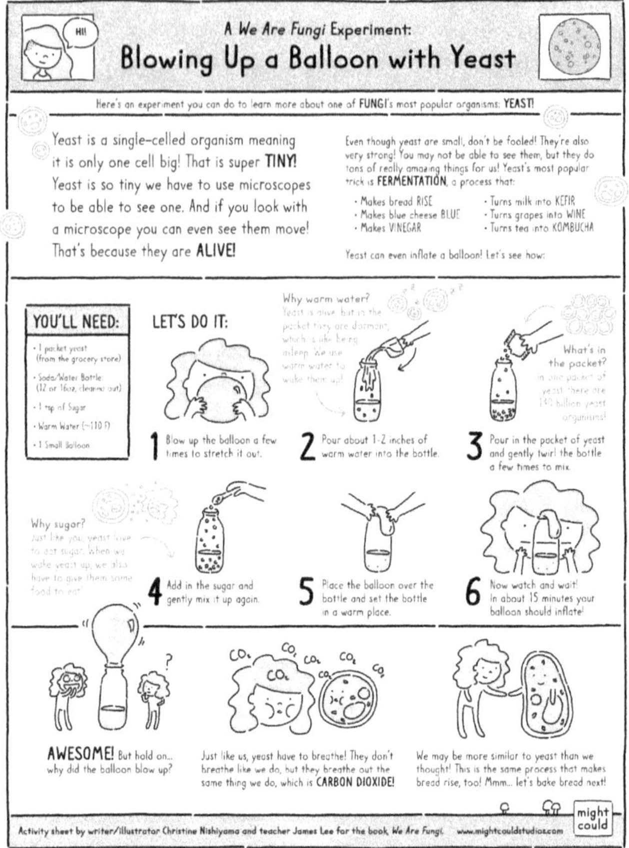

Activity Guides

Librarians, teachers, and parents love activity guides for children so having one available to download on your sales page can be a great way to bring people in! I teamed up with a friend of mine who was an elementary teacher to create a special fungi-related science activity to go with *We Are Fungi*. You can see that activity guide above and also on the sales page.

Social Media

I quit all social media in 2022, so I don't currently promote my books on Instagram, Facebook, TikTok, or whatever the kids are using these days. I could write a whole book on how quitting social media reoriented my art practice (and my life?) and how it was one of the best decisions I've made for myself. But that's not the book I'm writing here, now is it? If you want to read more about my thoughts on social media and how artists can still share their art and connect without it, read my essay on that here: *https://imightcoulddothat.substack.com/p/on-quitting-social-media-as-an-artist*

With that said, when I self-published *We Are Fungi* in 2017, I was still on Instagram and shared process shots and videos there. Some authors and illustrators choose to do whole marketing campaigns on social media, but my opinion is that takes up a whole lot of time for very minimal gains. The chance that someone is going to click a link on your Instagram post and buy your book is very low. These days, the chance many people will see your post at all is very low.

Personally, I prefer to focus my promotion on my email list as my email subscribers have opted in, receive 100% of what I share, are more invested in my work, and I have a direct link to them through their email inbox. Plus, I don't have to make dumb iPhone videos.

Am I an old crank? Maybe so. But I'm a heck of a lot happier off social media, and that's worth a few potential lost bucks, isn't it?

Amazon Author Central + Amazon Sales Page

If you're publishing through Amazon KDP or if your book will be sold on Amazon, it's a good idea to set up your Amazon Sales Page (for your book) and Author Central (for you). Amazon gives clear instructions on how to edit your sales page through Amazon KDP and connect it to your author's page, so I won't repeat that information here. (More on choosing where to self-publish in the next chapter.)

You can find a link to my Amazon pages on this book's resource page: *https://might-could.com/mcmb-resources/*

GoodReads Author Page

Similarly, you can set up your Author Page on Goodreads, the book reviewing website, so you are connected to your books there as well. You may start to get reviews on GoodReads and people can find you and your book there too!

You can find a link to my GoodReads Author page on this book's resource page: *https://might-could.com/mcmb-resources/*

CHAPTER 24

SELF-PUBLISHING OPTIONS

Distributor Or No?

There are tons of options for selling an indie book online. But the first thing you need to decide is whether you want to sell through a distributor or go at it alone.

Using A Distributor

Using a distributor mean selling your book through an existing platform like Amazon, Ingram, etc. The benefit of using a distributor is that they handle the distribution of the book. When a sale is made, you don't have to do anything—they handle the money, the printing, and shipping. You then get paid based on what sells.

The downside is that the distributor will take a cut of each sale. For example, Amazon KDP pays its authors a 60% royalty, meaning they take a 40% cut for themselves.

NOT Using A Distributor

If you don't use a distributor, you'll have to sell your book directly to your readers and handle the entire sales sequence. You will be responsible for processing payments, shipping books, and any resulting customer service. This could be done through your website using a service like Shopify, WooCommerce, or Gumroad.

The benefit to not using a distributor is you have complete control and don't have to share cuts of the sale (besides small fees to the point-of-sale service you choose). More control means you can decide exactly how your book is presented, sold, and retired. As an example, books printed through an outside distributor and sold on Amazon are notoriously difficult to remove from Amazon if you ever wish to stop selling it. If you are the distributor/seller, you can make those kinds of decisions and actions yourself without having to call or email an unresponsive customer service.

The downside to not using a distributor is each sale means more work for you. You have to handle the credit card payments, get the product in the hands of your customer, handle refunds and returns, etc. There are plenty of services to help automate this, but there will always be some extra tasks for you to do. You also have to bring in all readers yourself—there is no in-platform discovery like there might be on an existing platform like Amazon.

My Personal Preference

My personal preference is to use a distributor. An absurd percentage of all books are sold on Amazon, so why fight against that? I prefer not to do heavy marketing, so I like being able to be discovered on an existing platform like Amazon. And I would rather focus my time on making my next book, instead of customer service and product fulfillment. I'm willing to give up a little control and a slice of my profit for those benefits. You'll need to think about it and make your own decision!

Printing Options

There are two basic categories for printing a book: Digital Print-on-Demand and Offset Printing.

Digital Print-on-Demand (POD)

This method uses a printer similar to a home inkjet printer (albeit a very large one) where books are only printed as sales are made. POD allows you to upload your digital book files and then be mostly hands-off. When a sale is made, you don't have to do anything—the distributor handles the payment, production, and delivery. You get paid monthly royalties based on what is sold. Examples of POD printers include Amazon KDP, Lulu, and Ingram Spark.

One benefit of POD is that there's no up-front setup cost. It's free to upload your book files to a POD printer, and neither of you makes any money or incurs any costs until a book sale is made. Another benefit is there is no minimum book order. No books are printed until a book is sold, so you do not have to place a large book order to get the books printed (as is the case in offset). And with that, you as the author, do not have to store a large book order of 300 or more books. That's a garage full of books!

A drawback to POD is each book is more expensive to print. This means you will either need to raise the price of your book to give yourself a decent royalty, or be content with a lower profit per book. Some PODs also print at a lower-quality for ink, color, and paper. This varies from printer to printer and is not always a deal breaker. POD also gives less specialty printing options. You most likely won't be able to include designed end papers, or spot gloss or embossing on the cover.

Offset Printing

This method uses a large printing press with printing plates to print a bulk book order. Offset printing gives you the highest quality book, but requires a bulk order, usually 300+ books, and an upfront cost of thousands of dollars. An offset printer does not sell or distribute your books, they just print the entire book order and ship it to you. You must store, sell, and deliver the books yourself or use an additional service to do so. An example of an offset printer is PrintNinja, Ingram (they can do both), and local printers.

One benefit of offset printing is that they tend to produce higher quality books. They use premium inks, colors, and paper and have more options available for each. Because they print hundreds of books at once (instead of one at a time) each book typically costs less to produce. However this depends on the book. You also have more printing options with offset, including designed endpapers, paper choices, cover gloss, cover embossing, etc.

A major drawback to offset printing is the expensive upfront cost to the author. You must place a bulk order of 300+ to print your book offset, and you'll pay for them all at the time of order, potentially before you've sold any books. You may or may not sell all the books you ordered, and could potentially lose a lot of money. You'll also receive the entire book order at once and must have a way to store 300 books. That takes up more space than you think! You could use Amazon Warehouses, but that will cost you as well.

Financial Options for Bulk Orders

Print-on-demand requires no up-front cost. You only pay per book sold. Offset printing requires a bulk order to be placed, leaving you with an expensive up-front cost, and no guarantee those books will sell. So, if you want to offset, what can you do besides sink your entire savings account into a book order? (*Please* don't do that!)

Crowdfunding

Instead of emptying your bank account, you could try crowdfunding. This option allows you to test the waters for your book and receive funding for your upfront offset printing costs. It's a way to take pre-orders and guarantee you'll be able to make your money back *before* you pay for the bulk order of books.

However, crowdfunding is its own beast and can be very time-consuming and challenging. If you're not careful, you can sink more money and time into something that won't work or something that ends up burning you out.

To be honest, I've never run a successful crowdfunding campaign, so I don't have a ton of advice here. It is something I'm interested in experimenting with in the future thought. There are lots of guides and programs online with more guidance if you'd like to try crowdfunding. Examples include Kickstarter and IndieGoGo.

My Personal Choices

In my opinion, new authors should start with POD. It's not smart to sink your savings into a book you don't know will sell. Plus, 300 books take up *a lot* of space. My advice is to publish your first few books with POD until you have a good audience that you know will buy your books. Then maybe you can upgrade.

As for the distributor, I've used both Amazon KDP and Lulu, and my current preference is Amazon KDP. Their platform is easy to use, has lots of promotional features and printing options, and is continually adding new tools for self-publishers. Their customer service is also extremely prompt and helpful. In contrast, Lulu has not updated their products significantly in years, does not have nearly as helpful promotional tools, and their customer service is, in my experience, unresponsive.

CHAPTER 25

PRINTING + PUBLISHING SETUP

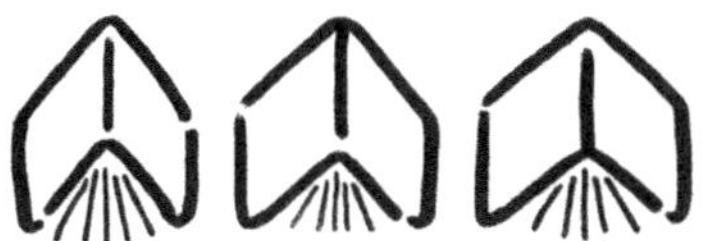

Finalize your book files

We're in the final countdown now! Complete one last check that everything is just how you want it in your book file. Read through everything and get a fresh pair of eyes to take a look too, if you can.

Buy your ISBN

Wait... what's an ISBN?

An ISBN (International Standard Book Number) is a number assigned to every published book. It includes information about the book like the title, publisher, and author, and is how a book is identified and cataloged by stores, distributors, and libraries.

Do I have to have an ISBN?

You need to have an ISBN if you intend to sell your book through any kind of book distributor (Amazon, Lulu, Ingram, etc.). Readers will also view your book as more professional if it has an ISBN. If you are working with a publisher, you don't have to worry about this. But if you're self-publishing, you are responsible for the ISBN.

If you want to go full indie and sell directly to your customers with no ISBN (perhaps selling at craft shows, local events, Gumroad, or your website), you can totally do that. Just know that without an ISBN, you won't be able to sell your book in bookstores or through a distributor.

Personally, I highly recommend getting an ISBN for your book. It's very easy to get one, it doesn't cost a whole lot, and it gives your book more options and more professionalism.

Where do I get an ISBN?

Option 1: Use a free ISBN from your distributor

Most self-publishing platforms, like Amazon KDP and Lulu, offer free ISBNs as part of publishing with them. They will assign an ISBN to your book and place it on your book cover for you.

The upside is it's free or at least very cheap. But the downside, is that you will not be listed as the publisher of your book. This means when your book is listed on Amazon or wherever you intend on selling it, the publisher will be listed at Amazon KDP or Lulu, or whichever platform you are using. That's may not be a big deal to everyone—as the author, you still own the book and copyright. But personally, I'd rather my books published in my studio's name.

Also keep in mind that your book will also always be associated with its publisher. This may matter down the line if you intend to try to get your book sold in bookstores that may not like to buy books published by Amazon! Or what if a smaller distributor like Lulu closes down? What happens to your book?

Option 2: Buy your own ISBN

The alternative is to buy your own ISBN through an ISBN service. The only official source of ISBNS in the United States is Bowker. You can buy one ISBN for $125, or ten ISBNs for $295. ISBNs never expire, so if you plan on making more books in the future, you'll save some money by buying in bulk. I bought ten when I published *We Are Fungi*, and have already used three!

The upside to buying your own ISBN is you will be listed everywhere as the publisher. Your book is not affiliated with any other publishing platform—only you and your business. The downside is it costs money. It's up to you if you think $125 is worth the book being published in your name. To me it is.

If you want to know more about ISBNs, Bowker has tons of great info on their website. You can find that link on the Resources page.

Upload your files to the publishing platform

Create and set up your account

This process will depend on what platform you choose, but they are mostly similar, and each platform should clearly explain what to do once you begin. You'll be asked to supply:

- **Title Info:** Title, author name, language, publication date
- **ISBN:** You just type in your ISBN and they place the image
- **Interior PDF:** Upload your the book file for your inside pages
    - Pay attention if the printer wants your PDF to be formatted in pages or spreads!
- **Cover PDF:** Upload your cover design
    - They will most likely want one cover image (front + back)
    - Use the printer's templates so the spine is the correct size based on the number of pages in your book. A link to this calculator is on the Resources page of this book.

Set your book price (and royalty amount)

When you submit your book you'll also need to choose a price. This will determine how much customers pay for your book and also therefore determine how much you make from each sale.

Most distributors pay out a royalty based on the book price after subtracting the printing cost. Amazon KDP currently pays a 60% royalty. Here is an example printing a 32 page color book at 8.5 in x 11 in with Amazon KDP and a list price of $14.99:

List price	Royalty Rate	Printing Cost	Royalty
$14.99	60%	$4.20	$4.79

In this case, your book would cost each customer $14.99 and you would receive $4.79 per book sold. The printing cost for this book is $4.20. This cost is based on page count, ink type (black or color, premium or standard), and trim size. Most distributors will give you a calculator to determine your paperback and hardcover printing cost, minimum list price, and royalties. I've listed Amazon KDP's calculator on the Resources page of this book.

Submit your files for review

Press that submit button! The publishing platform will review your files for any issues or missed requirements and most will get back to you with a book proof within 24 hours.

Review your book proof

The platform will require that you review a proof of your book, and some may require that you order and review a printed proof. It's a good idea to order and review a printed proof even if they don't require it to ensure everything prints out how you want it to! You'll just have to pay the base printing cost of your printed proof. My proof of *We Are Fungi* was $3.79.

Be sure you set up your files and order your proof with plenty of time before your launch date if you have one in mind. It should arrive within a week, but things can go wrong! If something is needs to be fixed from your proof you'll need to change it, re-upload the edited file, and possibly order another proof.

Approving your book proof

Once you're happy with the proof, click approve! The timing until your book is available for sale will depend on the platform you choose and is a little variable. Amazon KDP says once you approve the proof, your book will be available for purchase on Amazon in 3-5 business days. For *We Are Fungi,* it was available after 1 business day. They are constantly adding new features here for authors and just released a way for you to set a manual release date.

CHAPTER 26

BOOK LAUNCH PROMOTION

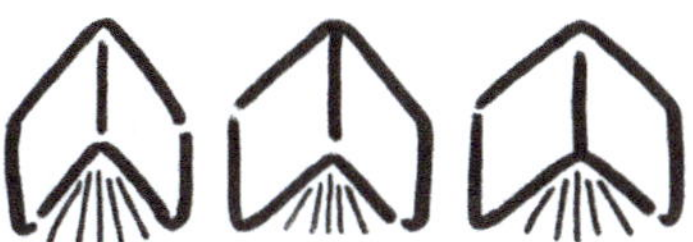

Photograph Your Book

It's important to have professional-looking photos of your book for your website's sales page. You can do this as soon as you get your printed proof before the book is officially published!

My go-to method is to place a big white sheet of paper on the ground outside or by a very sunny window and photograph the cover and interior spreads that way. Metal clamps can help you hold open the spreads, or you can ask a friend to hold the book. Sunlight is generally better for product photos than artificial light, unless you have fancy photographer lights.

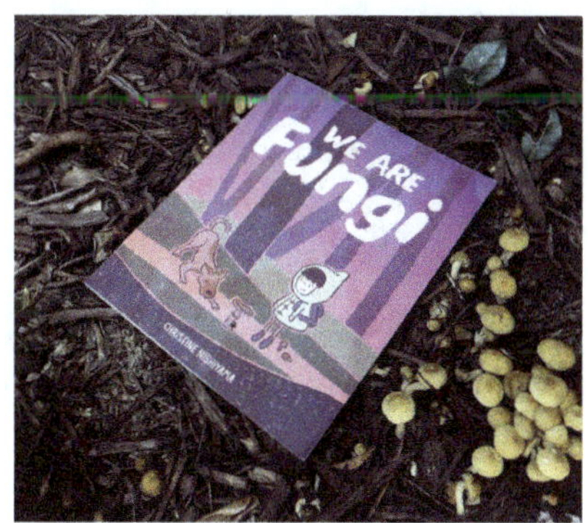

You can edit your photos in Photoshop or software of your choice, removing the background, adjusting the levels, etc. I like to have at least two versions of the cover and each spread: one on a plain white background and one on a more fun/related to the topic background (like mushrooms!).

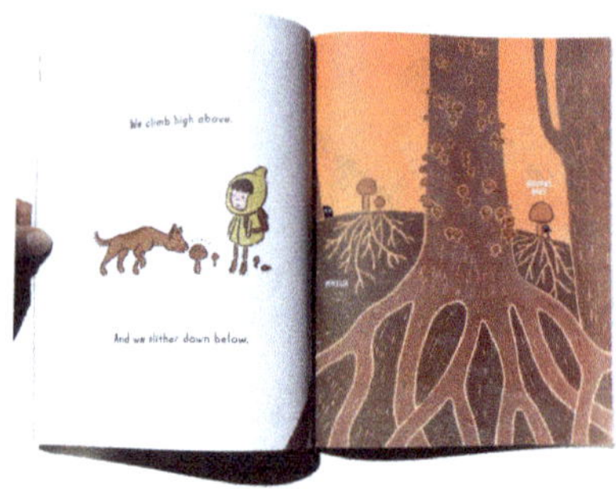

Book Launch Day Tasks

Don't sleep on launch day! On the day your book goes live and is available for purchase, you've got some work to do. Particularly if you are selling your book on Amazon. If you have a wave of people clicking on and looking (and buying!) your book in the first few days, Amazon will push it up its lists and promote it to other people as well. So we might as well try!

Sales Page

Make sure the buttons on your website's sales page link to where to buy the book. Consider adding a smart bar or pop-up on your website to alert visitors that your book is now launched! If you have the ability to, you could choose to offer a special deal for launch day.

Email Campaign

Send out your book launch day email you planned in Chapter 23. Announce that the book is now live and include some fun photos of the book. Link to your sales page and/or where they can buy the book and ask them to share the link with friends!

Social Media

I'm not going to repeat my rant about social media here (you can find it in Chapter 23). You should focus your time online wherever you feel gives you the most value—and I mean that not only in terms of sales, but also everything else you value. In my opinion, social media does not bring in as many sales as some people say it does, and I also just don't *like* it and don't find *value* in it, so I don't do it!

When *We Are Fungi* was published, I was still on Medium and Instagram. I wrote a couple essays about the book-making process on Medium during launch week and posted about once a day on Instagram for the week of the launch, sharing behind-the-scenes tidbits about the book.

For this book you are reading, I was/am not on social media, so I focused all my promotion on my Substack email newsletter. This is a platform I like and find value in (it favors long-form writing, artistic voice, genuine connection, and has no ads or algorithms!).

Advertising

Some authors choose to run online ads for their books, but that, like crowdfunding is a whole other beast that I don't know much about. It seems to me that perhaps the days of running successful online ads are also shrinking. It's possible you'll make some sales from ads, but it's also possible you'll waste your time and money.

Personally, I believe organic reach is more powerful than advertising to strangers. It's the long game, but making books is my career, not a one-off, so the long game is worth it to me. But that's just me. If you want to try ads, then go for it!

Giveaways

Instead of ads, a Giveaway can be an alternative promotional tactic. It's extremely cheap (compared to ads), you just have to pay the printing cost of each book you give away (which was $4 for me). I chose to run a giveaway for one copy of *We Are Fungi* through Amazon. To enter the giveaway, a person just had to follow my Amazon Author Page and then click the giveaway link provided.

This promotion was awesome because it promoted my book while also getting people to follow my Author Page. So the next time I publish a book on Amazon, those people will automatically get a notification about it! While only one person received the book from the giveaway, I got a slight uptick in book sales during the giveaway, so I assume many of the people who didn't win decided to buy the book anyway! Amazon KDP is consistently adding more tools like this to their platform.

CHAPTER 27

YOU MADE A BOOK!

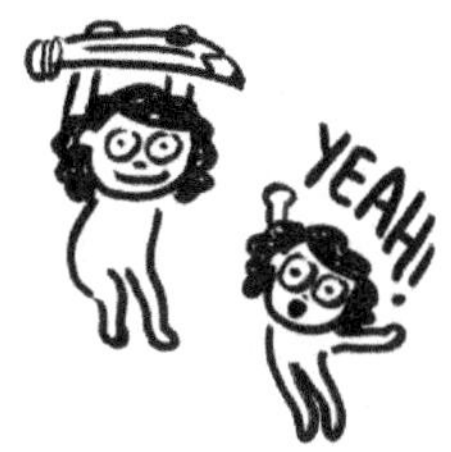

Wee-woo! Congratulations!

Or... wait. Did you just read this book and you haven't actually done anything towards making your book yet? Don't worry, I get it. I went through that period too, reading everything I could about making books but not actually, you know, making books.

Well I'm here right now to give you a little kick in the booty—start making your book! You obviously have an idea for a picture book or you wouldn't be reading this. So what are you waiting for? More information? More instructions? More steps to follow? You've got everything you need right now to get started! I've shown you how I made my book and how a book is generally made, but I can't tell you how to make *your* book. Only you can figure that out. And the only way you can do that is to just start making it.

I believe making art is one of the best ways we can spend our time, and there's not much better than seeing your idea come to life.

So c'mon baby, *you might could make a book!*

Thank you!

Thank you so much for reading this book and I hope it helped you on your bookmaking journey!

I would love to connect more with you and see any finished or in-progress books you're making! If you're interested, you can join my email newsletter at the URL below, which includes weekly essays on creativity, drawing prompts, and behind-the-scenes process work of my current books:

https://might-could.com/emails

You can also email me if you have questions about book making or would like to share your book with me—I'd love to read it and share it once it's published!

christine@mightcouldstudios.com

Welp, that wraps it all up—I really hope you enjoyed Might Could Make a Book! Don't forget to check out the Resources in the next pages and the Resources webpage, which includes all the links and digital files that pair with this book.

Thank you again and best of luck with your book!

<3,
Christine Nishiyama

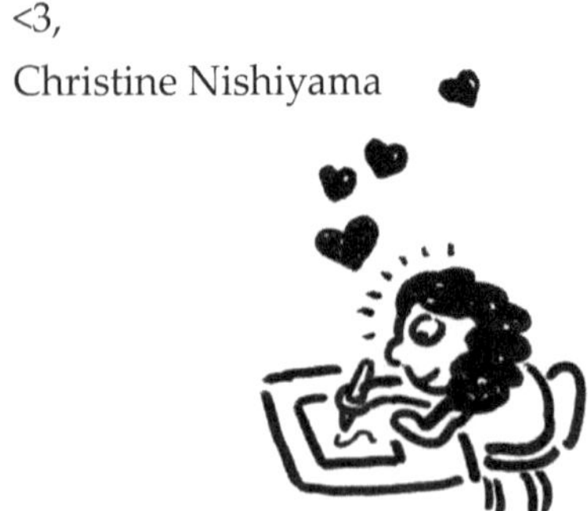

RESOURCES

Resources Webpage

Here are some extra links and templates to help you as you begin making your picture book. At the website below, you can find all the links listed in this book, storyboard templates, break-downs of my writing and drawing processes, a video showing every step of making *We Are Fungi*, and more!

Check out the resources here:
https://might-could.com/mcmb-resources/

Join my email list here:
www.might-could.com/emails

Read my Substack publication, *I Might Could Do That*:
https://imightcoulddothat.substack.com/

FURTHER READING

On Writing for Children

- *Writing Picture Books,* by Ann Whitford Paul
- *Caldecott and Co.: Notes on Books and Pictures,* by Maurice Sendak
- *Children's Picturebooks: The Art of Visual Storytelling,* by Martin Salisbury and Morag Styles

On Writing

- *Bird by Bird: Some Instructions on Writing and Life,* by Anne Lamott
- *On Writing: A Memoir of the Craft,* by Stephen King
- *On Writing Well: The Classic Guide to Writing Nonfiction,* William Zinsser
- *What I Talk About When I Talk About Running,* by Haruki Murakami
- *Zen in the Art of Writing: Releasing the Creative Genius Within You,* by Ray Bradbury

On Poetry

- *A Child's Anthology of Poetry,* by Elizabeth Hauge Sword
- *A Child's Book of Poems,* by Gyo Fujikawa

On Storytelling

- *The Storytelling Animal: How Stories Make Us Human,* by Jonathan Gottschall
- *The Hero with a Thousand Faces,* by Joseph Campbell

On Creativity

- *Big Magic: Creative Living Beyond Fear,* by Elizabeth Gilbert
- *Steal Like an Artist: 10 Things Nobody Told You about Being Creative,* by Austin Kleon
- *What It Is,* by Lynda Barry
- *Art & Fear: Observations on the Perils (and Rewards) of Artmaking,* by Ted Orland and David Bayles
- *The Artist's Way,* by Julia Cameron
- *Understanding Comics: The Invisible Art,* by Scott McCloud

Classic Children's Books to Study

- *The Tale of Peter Rabbit,* by Beatrix Potter (1902)
- *Runaway Bunny,* by Margaret Wise Brown and Clement Moore (1942)
- *The Little Prince,* by Antoine de Saint-Exupéry (1943)
- *The Book about Moomin, Mymble and Little My,* by Tove Jansson (1952)
- *Madeline's Rescue,* by Ludwig Bemelmans (1954)
- *This Is...* series, by M. Sasek (1959–1974)
- *The Cat in the Hat,* by Dr. Seuss (1957)
- *Are You My Mother?,* by P.D. Eastman (1960)
- *The Snowy Day,* by Ezra Jack Keats (1962)

- *Where the Wild Things Are,* by Maurice Sendak (1963)
- *Best Word Book Ever,* by Richard Scarry (1963)
- *Babies,* by Gyo Fujikawa (1963)
- *The Giving Tree,* by Shel Silverstein (1964)
- *Charlie and the Chocolate Factory,* by Roald Dahl (1964)
- *Corduroy,* by Don Freeman (1968)
- *The Very Hungry Caterpillar,* by Eric Carle (1969)
- *Miss Nelson Is Missing!,* by Harry Allard and James Marshall (1973)
- *Strega Nona,* by Tomie dePaola (1975)
- *Moo Baa La La La,* by Sandra Boynton (1982)
- *A Visit to William Blake's Inn: Poems for Innocent and Experienced Travelers,* Nancy Willard and Alice and Martin Provensen (1982)
- *The Napping House,* by Audrey Wood and Don Wood (1984)
- *If You Give a Mouse a Cookie,* by Laura Numeroff and Felicia Bond (1985)
- *The Polar Express,* by Chris Van Allsburg (1985)
- The *Jolly Postman,* by Janet and Allan Ahlberg (1986)
- *Goldilocks and the Three Bears,* by Jan Brett (1987)
- *The True Story of the Three Little Pigs,* by Jon Scieszka and Lane Smith (1989)
- *The Rainbow Fish,* by Marcus Pfister (1992)
- *Good night, Gorilla,* by Peggy Rathmann (1994)
- *Brown Bear, Brown Bear, What Do You See?,* by Bill Martin, Jr and Eric Carle (1996)
- *Rapunzel,* by Paul O. Zelinsky (1997)
- *Click, Clack, Moo,* by Doreen Cronin and Betsy Lewin (2000)

Contemporary Children's Books to Study

- *The Three Pigs,* by David Wiesner (2001)
- *My Friend Rabbit,* by Eric Rohmann (2002)
- *Don't Let the Pigeon Drive the Bus,* by Mo Willems (2003)
- *Llama Llama Red Pajama,* by Anna Dewdney (2005)
- *A Couple of Boys Have the Best Week Ever,* by Marla Frazee (2008)
- *A Sick Day for Amos McGee,* by Philip C. Stead and Erin E. Stead (2010)
- *I Want My Hat Back,* by Jon Klassen (2011)
- *Goodnight, Goodnight Construction Site,* by Sherri Duskey Rinker and Tom Lichtenheld (2011)
- *Press Here,* by Herve Tullet (2011)
- *Creepy Carrots!,* by Aaron Reynolds and Peter Brown (2012)
- *Dragons Love Tacos,* by Adam Rubin and Daniel Salmieri (2012)
- *Rabbit's Snow Dance,* Joseph Bruchac, James Bruchac
- and Jeff Newman (2012)
- *The Day the Crayons Quit,* by Drew Daywalt and Oliver Jeffers (2013)
- *Journey,* by Aaron Becker (2013)
- *Locomotive,* by Brian Floca (2013)
- *Ball,* by Mary Sullivan (2013)
- *Feathers: Not Just for Flying,* by Melissa Stewart and Sarah S. Brannen (2014)
- *The Adventures of Beekle: The Unimaginary Friend,* by Dan Santat (2014)
- *Last Stop on Market Street,* by Matt de la Peña and Christian Robinson (2015)
- *Wolfie the Bunny,* by Ame Dyckman and Zachariah OHora (2015)
- *They All Saw a Cat,* by Brendan Wenzel (2016)

- *Big Cat, Little Cat,* by Elisha Cooper (2017)
- *The Bad Seed,* by Jory John and Pete Oswald (2017)
- *Hello Lighthouse,* by Sophie Blackall (2018)
- *Julián is a Mermaid,* by Jessica Love (2018)
- *A Big Mooncake for Little Star,* by Grace Lin (2018)
- *Thank You, Omu!,* by Oge Mora (2018)
- *When Sadness is at Your Door,* by Eva Eland (2019)
- *Another,* by Christian Robinson (2019)
- *Elvis Is King!,* by Jonah Winter and Red Nose Studio (2019)
- *My Papi Has a Motorcyle,* by Isabel Quintero and Zeke Peña (2019)
- *Pokko and the Drum,* by Matthew Forsythe (2019)
- *Crab Cake: Turning the Tide Together,* by Andrea Tsurumi (2019)
- *Ten Ways to Hear Snow,* by Cathy Camper (2020)
- *Honeybee: The Busy Life of Apis Mellifera,* by Candace Fleming and Eric Rohmann (2020)
- *I Talk Like a River,* by Jordan Scott and Sydney Smith (2020)
- *Our Little Kitchen,* by Jillian Tamaki (2020)
- *Chez Bob,* by Bob Shea (2021)
- *Little Witch Hazel: A Year in the Forest,* by Phoebe Wahl (2021)
- *How to Say Hello to a Worm,* Kari Percival (2022)
- *Hot Dog,* by Doug Salati (2022)
- *John's Turn,* by Mac Barnett and Kate Berube (2022)
- *Love in the Library,* by Maggie Tokuda-Hall and Yas Imamura (2022)
- *Rick the Rock of Room 214,* by Julie Falatko and Ruth Chan (2022)
- *Oh, Panda,* by Cindy Derby (2023)
- *Ancient Night,* by David Álvarez with David Bowles (2023)
- *Big,* by Vashti Harrison (2023)

TEMPLATES

Storyboard Templates

In the following pages you'll find my storyboard templates for use with your own book. You can photocopy these pages, draw your own from this design, or download the digital files at the book resources webpage and then print them out as large as possible. *(https://might-could.com/mcmb-resources/)*

There are three basic page layout options: landscape, portrait, or square. The choice is up to you, and it's worth experimenting with different ones!

Portrait Storyboard

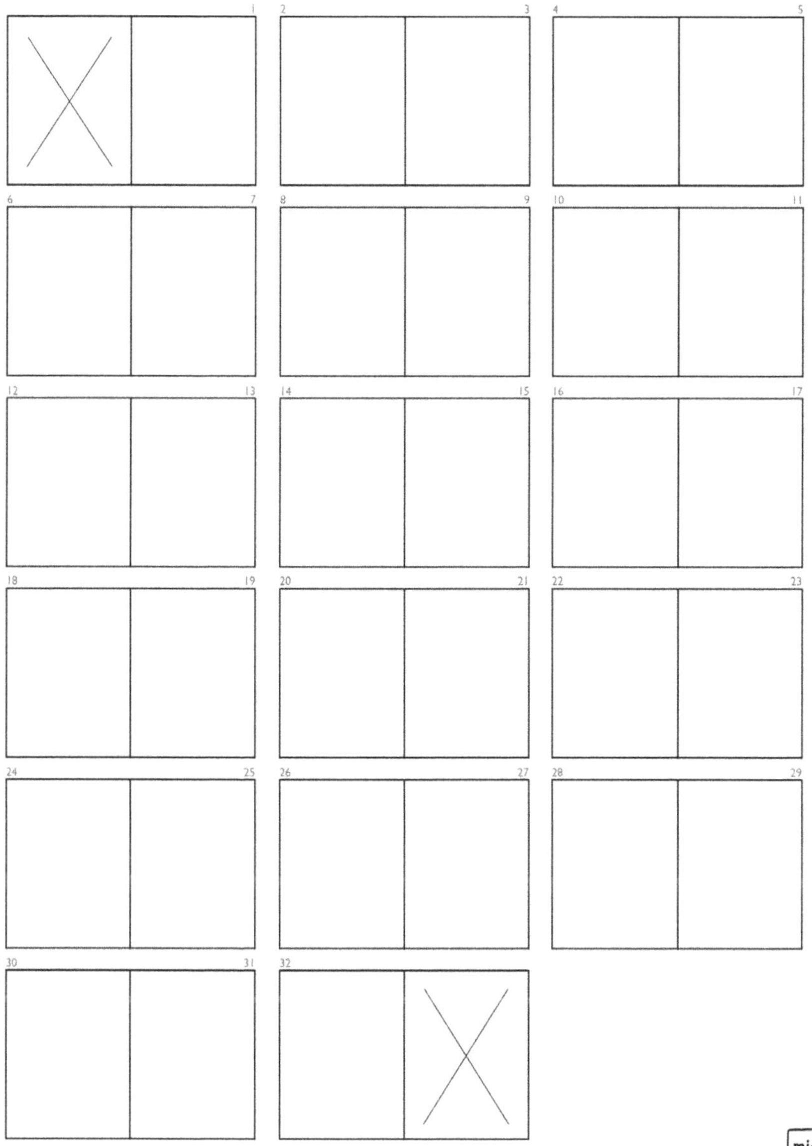

Storyboard Template created by Christine Nishiyama for her book: Might Could Make a Book

might could

Square Storyboard

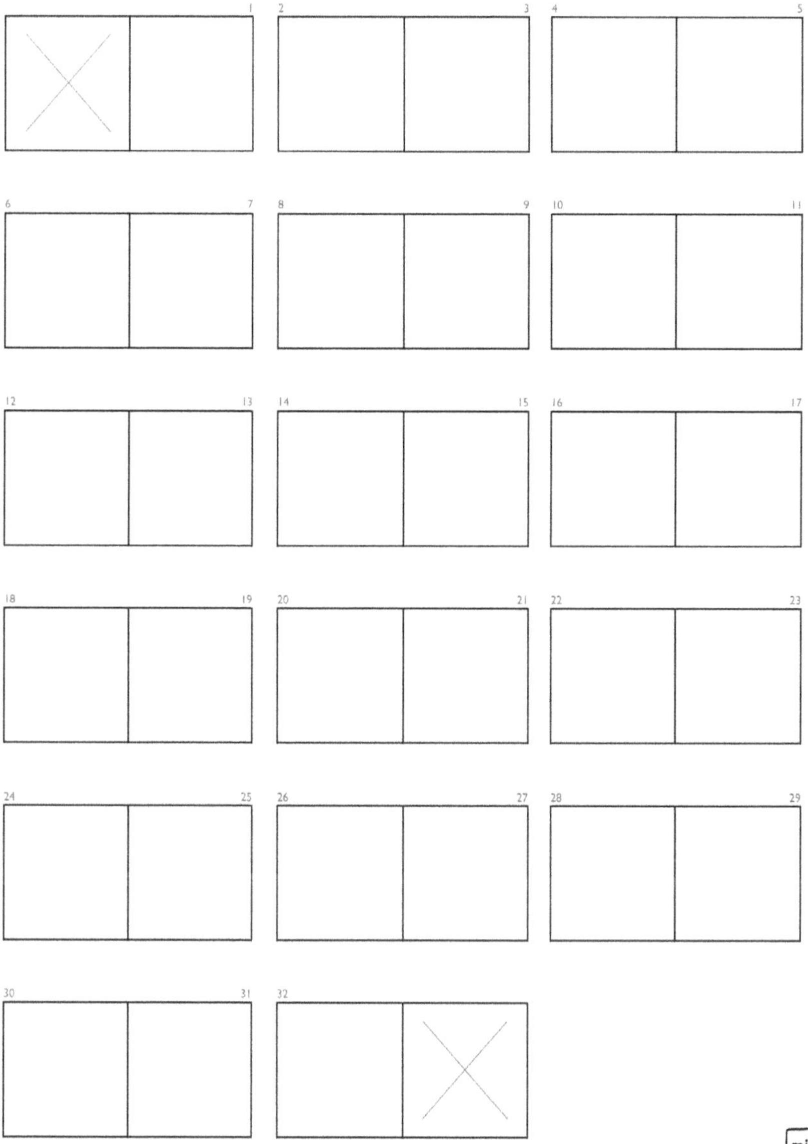

1 | 2 3 | 4 5

6 7 | 8 9 | 10 11

12 13 | 14 15 | 16 17

18 19 | 20 21 | 22 23

24 25 | 26 27 | 28 29

30 31 | 32

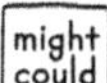

Storyboard Template created by Christine Nishiyama for her Might Could Beta Books initiative

Landscape Storyboard

Storyboard Template created by Christine Nishiyama for her Might Could Beta Books initiative

might could

About the Author

Christine Nishiyama is the author and/or illustrator of seven books, including the 4-book *Layla and the Bots* series published by Scholastic. She also self-published the indie picture book, *We Are Fungi.* Besides making books, she also writes weekly essays for her email newsletter and teaches online classes with more than 100,000 students. She lives high up in the beautiful Blue Ridge Mountains of western North Carolina with her husband, daughter, and grumpy old dog. She believes making art is one of the best ways a person can spend their time and has dedicated her life to doing so and helping others do the same. Please visit her online at ***www.might-could.com***

www.ingramcontent.com/pod-product-compliance
Lightning Source LLC
LaVergne TN
LVHW010902110826
845149LV00005B/1444
9780999403921